PERFECT
MEETING

Terry O'Brien is a best-selling author, columnist, consultant and motivational trainer. He is highly sought-after in the corporate as well as academic world, and has been training managers and providing counselling and consultancy over the past couple of decades. Author of hugely popular books on motivation, effective change and all that is 'un-Google-able', his writings focus on skill development and communication techniques. Terry O'Brien is a firm believer that 'infotainment' is a must for content to be effective, and his books are all about the three 'R's: Read, Record and Recall.

PERFECT
MEETING

Get it right every time

Terry O'Brien

RUPA

Published by
Rupa Publications India Pvt. Ltd 2017
7/16, Ansari Road, Daryaganj
New Delhi 110002

Sales centres:
Allahabad Bengaluru Chennai
Hyderabad Jaipur Kathmandu
Kolkata Mumbai

ISBN: 978-81-291-4541-3

First impression 2017

10 9 8 7 6 5 4 3 2 1

Typeset by Chetan Sharma

Contents

Introduction

Meetings are important for building rapport. In fact, they are great for building supportive relationships. They are a forum for inter-learning and understanding. They're vital for learning about our colleagues' motivations, fears, hopes and troubles, and not to just communicate but also read faces. It is the time for us to go beyond emails and reports. It is the best platform to share information.

A team meeting is a level playing field and an open forum—everybody present shares the same opportunity to communicate and listen. Meetings play a vital role in leadership—the team leader can rally the members and remind attendees of the mission and vision. Nothing can replace the closeness, security and intimacy of a team meeting, especially in times of crisis. Team meeting is a time above rote applications; it allows attendees to lift themselves above day-to-day operations. Team meetings are a learning and improvement opportunity. They're a great reminder that we are in fact in a team—and not alone! And the best part is feedback. They create a space for giving/receiving feedback.

No organisation can really function without meetings. After all, how else does one department communicate with another? How, indeed, do colleagues discuss shared problems and their possible solutions? Whether a regular, formal event or a more ad hoc arrangement, meetings should always be an integral part of professional life.

With the global trend away from an industrial economy (with fewer decision-makers and more 'doers') towards an information/service-based economy (where localised decision-making is a daily necessity), meetings now provide a more significant employee participation than ever before.

This book showcases how any meeting can be conducted in a way that it enriches the experience and skills of its participants, generating cooperation and commitment to achieve higher levels of performance.

The emphasis of this book is on the basic skills of management and it makes little claim to originality or depth; it is based on the premise of experience and learning.

Indeed, here is all you need to get it right every time!

Introduction

Meetings are important for building a rapport. In fact, they are great for building supportive relationships. They are a forum for inter-learning and understanding. They're vital for learning about our colleagues' motivations, fears, hopes and troubles, and not to just communicate but also read faces. It is the time for us to go beyond emails and reports. It is the best platform to share information.

A team meeting is a level playing field and an open forum—everybody present shares the same opportunity to communicate and listen. Meetings play a vital role in leadership—the team leader can rally the members and remind attendees of the mission and vision. Nothing can replace the closeness, security and intimacy of a team meeting, especially in times of crisis. Team meeting is a time above rote applications; it allows attendees to lift themselves above day-to-day operations. Team meetings are a learning and improvement opportunity. They're a great reminder that we are in fact in a team—and not alone! And the best part is the feedback. They create a space for giving each other feedback.

No organisation can really function without meetings. After all, how else does one department communicate with another? How, indeed, do colleagues discuss shared problems and their possible solutions? Whether a regular, formal event or a more ad hoc arrangement, meetings should always be an integral part of working life.

With the global trend away from an industrial economy (with fewer decision-makers and more 'doers') towards an information/service-based economy (where localised decision-making is a daily necessity), meetings now provide a more significant employee participation than ever before.

This book will show how any meeting can be conducted in such a way that it enriches the working of its participants, generating cooperation and commitment to higher levels of performance.

The emphasis of this book is on the basic skill of management. It makes little claim to originality or depth. It is a book that is based on the premise of experience and learning.

Effective Meetings

There are good meetings and there are bad meetings. Bad meetings seem to go on forever, and you leave wondering why you were even present in the first place. Effective ones leave you energised and feeling that you've accomplished something.

Benefits of increasing effectiveness of meetings

- Reduce stress—you will get more done, in less time, with less effort.

- This will accelerate innovation; you will increase the quality, volume and frequency of your strategic insight.

- This will increase speed to deliver; you will respond more quickly to organisational needs and opportunities.

- This will decrease cost; you will likely reduce the number of meetings and, in doing so, will dramatically reduce direct and indirect costs.

- This will increase engagement and teamwork; you will create meetings that people want to attend, and they will bring greater levels of commitment every day.

- Reinforce desired ethos and organisational culture. It will spread multiple dimensions, energy and optimism in your organisation.

- This will increase accountability; it will bring about a sense of belonging to the organisation and be part of its vision, mission and value statements.

- This will provide a sense of purpose.

- This will accelerate towards your aspirations; you will direct all available energy towards your goals.

PLANNING FOR A MEETING

To fail to prepare is to prepare to fail. So we need to hear the warning bell.

- How many meetings do you turn up at totally unprepared?

- With twenty minutes in hand, you can do several things before a meeting.

Here is **one key** thing to do just twenty minutes before a meeting to give you a chance to have a meaningful and result-oriented meeting.

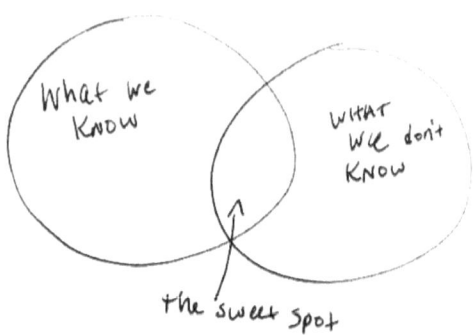

TWENTY MINUTES BEFORE A MEETING

- *Check the location:* Where is the conference/the meeting room? Check where it is in case you've got to time yourself to be there on time.

- *Check the agenda:* Make brief notes. Yes, you need to familiarise yourself with the agenda for this particular meeting.

- *Check the attendees:* If possible find out absentees, if any. Microsoft Outlook gives you the data to see who has responded and who has declined.

- *Check the 'inputs' annexures/documents:* Take a printout. Don't simply have it on your laptop.

- *Check previous action taken:* Action taken report is very helpful to evaluate where matters stand.

- *Check your calendar:* Now, look where you need to be after this meeting, and if necessary gather any inputs for that meeting too.

- *Check your email:* Do this before rather than during the meeting on your smart phone!

- *Check if the meeting is still on:* Meetings can be cancelled at the last minute; check that it is still on.

- *Visit the restroom.*

- *Get your beverage:* If you need a fix, get your beverage.

PLANNING FOR PEOPLE

As chairperson, an important part of your preparation involves thinking through the proposed meeting long before it takes place. In other words, exploring all the possibilities, understanding and identifying possible stick points could help one pre-empt them.

By considering the probable needs, wants and motivations of the participants, you will be able to estimate the likely course of the meeting and can approach it more comprehensively.

Questions to help your preparation

- Who will be at the meeting?

- What are the participants particularly concerned about, or interested in?

- What are their individual aims, aspirations and assumptions about the meeting—particularly where contentious issues are likely to arise?

- How do you envisage reconciling these individual aims, aspirations and assumptions into a coherent whole?

- Who has the authority to get things done?

- What are your priorities for achieving the desired outcomes—and what particular issues might get in the way of you achieving them?

- How can you ensure that all those participating prepare effectively for the meeting?

Relevant Information To Members

Obviously, as chairperson, you must familiarise yourself with any meeting papers or relevant information sent out with the agenda. Less obviously, but equally important, you must encourage everyone participating in the meeting to do their 'homework'.

One way of doing this is to get into the habit of starting the meeting with the clear assumption that everyone is properly prepared. Participants will quickly understand that valuable time will not be devoted to debating minor details of pre-meeting papers—or demotivating those who have prepared diligently by reiterating information for those who haven't!

Preparation Checklist

When you come to prepare for a meeting, make sure you have allowed time for the following.

- Doing your own 'homework' on the agenda
- Notifying all participants in good time
- Making sure that all who are invited can attend
- Making sure that the meeting room is ready
- Making sure that participants have enough time to meet any special technical needs for the meeting—visual aids, presentations, etc.

Venue

Do make sure that someone visits the venue before the meeting to check its suitability. If there are doubts about the number of participants, you should aim for a degree of flexibility in the layout. Can unnecessary furniture or fittings be removed to create more space, for instance? If the venue does prove to be unsuitable, you must have enough time to organise an alternative.

It is also important to run through a checklist of the facilities that the venue has available.

- Are there enough chairs?

- Does it have any tables, audio-visual equipment or overhead projectors, etc., that you may require?

- If you need to bring your own audio-visual equipment, are there enough accessible power points for it?

- Who will be in charge of the booking and maintenance of such equipment?

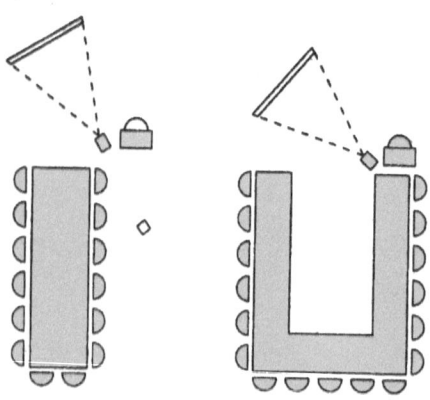

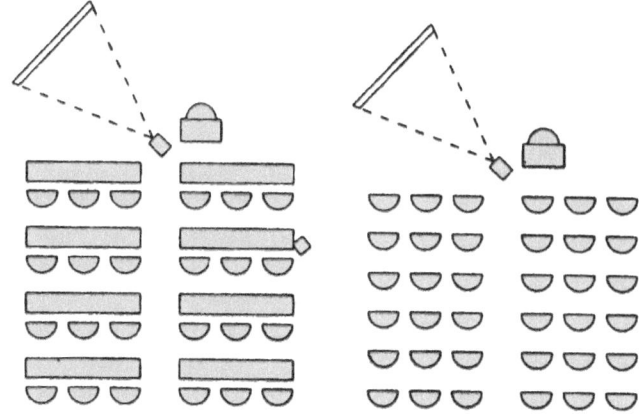

- Because of the set-up of the room, are there likely to be distractions—trains passing close by, orchestra rehearsals, etc.—at particular times of the day?

- Is there adequate heating, lighting and ventilation for the type of meeting you are holding?

Planning Room Layout

Every effort should be made to ensure that the room layout is conducive to good contact between all the participants. Everyone should be able to see and hear each other clearly. The room should be large enough to hold the meeting in comfort, but make sure that participants don't feel distanced from each other.

Comfortable chairs also have a significant role to play—particularly in a long meeting. After all, you want people to be concentrating on the matter in hand, not shifting in their seats, trying to restore the circulation to their aching behinds!

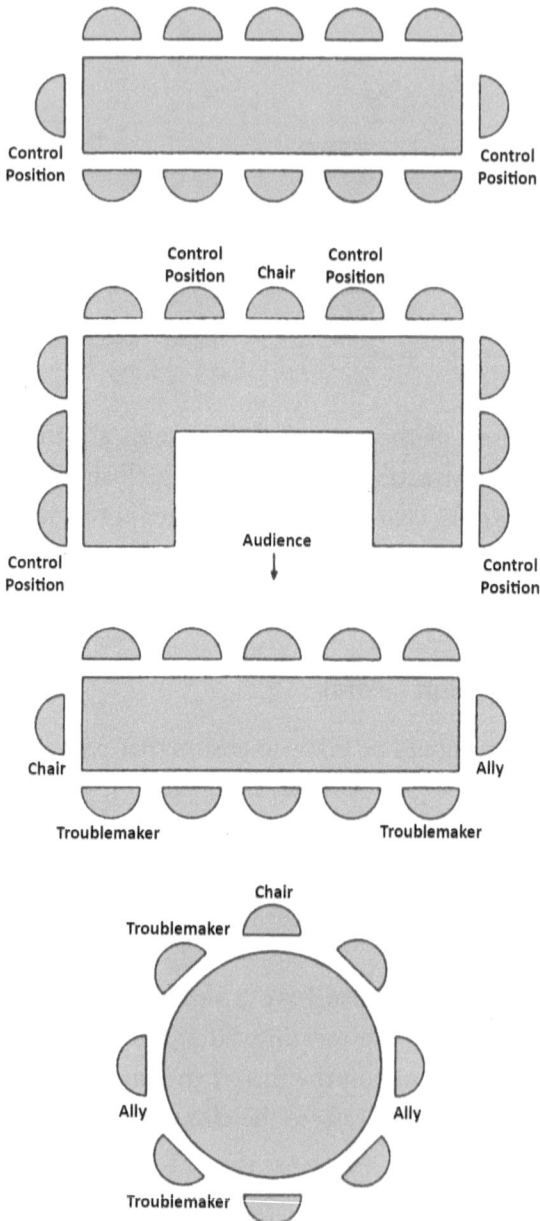

With a bit of thought, it can be relatively easy to adapt an existing layout to suit your purposes. First, you must put fixtures, fittings and furniture into the following categories.

- Fixed—for instance, the walls, which tend to be permanent

- Semi-fixed—partitions or platforms

- Flexible—chairs and tables, projectors, televisions (unless wall-bracketed) and other audio-visual equipment

Note: The most common mistake is treating semi-fixed items as if they are fixed, thereby losing an opportunity to alter the arrangement of the room quickly and easily.

Seating Plan

As chairperson, you must be able to make contact with all participants at any point in the meeting. You will, therefore, need to be in a central position so that you can see everyone and keep a firm grip on guiding the meeting.

Depending on the shape of the table, different seating positions allow the chairperson to make a greater impact. For instance, if you anticipate conflict, it is helpful to have potential rivals on either side of you rather than facing each other.

Quantitative input/output and focus on the achievement of organisational results

Hindsight: Manage Backwards

This type of meeting is where you and your manager review work already carried out since your last meeting. It will tend to be data-driven. Review if targets have been met, or not. You may have Key Performance Indicators (KPIs) that you and your manager will discuss, be it, under-performance or over-performance, in order to ensure the level of achievement. Your manager may reward or penalise you. You might also review a to-do list which defines specific objectives.

Forward Strategy: Manage Forward

This is where you and your manager look ahead at work to be carried out by your next meeting. You may use analytics and other data to forecast future achievement of performance targets and make adjustments accordingly, which could be funding, resourcing and/or prioritisation. You might also create or add to a to-do list which defines specific objectives.

Highlight Change: Lead Backwards

This type of meeting involves reviewing change and how it was brought about, since your last meeting. You and your manager will review what went well and what didn't, from a behavioural perspective. You may review how you achieved specific change goals. This meeting should focus on the competencies and processes you used, to deliver the required change.

Move Ahead: Lead Forward

This is where you and your manager agree on the changes you will make and how to make them happen, before your next meeting. You may agree on which personal and organisational behaviours you intend to change, and how. Your manager may use this meeting to inspire and motivate you towards these goals, and you may discuss the competencies and processes required to deliver the required change.

AGENDA

If you hold meetings, then you need an agenda. This sets a positive goal.

A meeting agenda is a powerful tool to ensure that your meeting achieves its aim. Today, however, organisations/ modern businesses are plagued by a fixation on meetings. Meetings are held, week in, week out, without a clear purpose, without a clear agenda. Agendas help steer a meeting effectively towards the goal, but first, we have to know what that goal is. Here are some steps to follow.

Step One: Be Clear About The Purpose Of The Meeting

If this isn't clear, then cancel the meeting straight-away! Our meetings must have a desired outcome: agreement on an action, making a decision and communicate change. The purpose should be easy to articulate and specific enough so that all attendees know what it's about. For example:

'Bad' purpose: Listen to what people have to say about the product.

'Good' purpose: Gather feedback about the issue, and then agree upon a list of prioritised actions to be performed by the team.

'Bad' purpose: To share information about team activity.

'Good' purpose: To monitor team activities and agree upon any management interventions required.

Step Two: Create The Agenda

Once you are crystal clear about what your meeting is for, you can begin to put the agenda together. Your agenda should have these components.

- Date, time and location
- Attendees and other participants
- Absentees/Apologies–it's always helpful to find out who won't be there, as this may cause the meeting to be postponed.

Agenda, to include:

- Agenda item (title and description)
- 'Inputs'—any documentation to be used in the agenda item
- Desired outcome (decision, action or sharing information)
- Agenda item duration
- Agenda item owner(s)
- Chairperson
- Minute taker (see minute-taking made easy)—to be agreed upfront

DISTRIBUTING YOUR AGENDA

Do distribute your agenda as soon as you can. This is necessary for the following reasons.

- It gives people enough time to prepare their agenda items, inputs and any supporting material.

- It gives people a chance to challenge the agenda, its purpose and participants.

- It allows people to consider the appropriateness of the meeting without absent attendees.

- It allows enough time to get the meeting into attendees' diaries.

Not all meetings require a formal agenda; nevertheless, an emergency meeting still needs a purpose. These meetings work well when everything above holds true, even if it's communicated quickly in a few statements. For meetings to be effective, participants need time to prepare and get into the 'zone' of the meeting, i.e. putting aside current tasks so they can focus on the meeting.

MINUTES

There comes a time, when it becomes important to take the 'minutes' of a meeting. In fact, they are an important record of a meeting, and getting it right is crucial—or we spend more time trying to remember what was said and who said it, in the next meeting.

Remember: Minute-taking isn't one of those things that is taught in education.

Minute-taking

In its simplest form, minute-taking is making a record of discussion, decisions and actions to be taken and the date by when these need to be completed.

The minutes are not a blow-by-blow transcript of the whole conversation—their purpose is to ensure that any agreements and actions are captured so that the people, who took responsibility for them, have something to refer back to.

General process of taking minutes

- Start of meeting—person taking the minutes is registered with the attendees, and then attendees are noted (and anyone missing recorded—often tagged as 'apologies'). The start time of the meeting is recorded in the minutes.

- The minutes of the previous meeting are reviewed and actions/updates reported and recorded in the minutes.

- Whenever a discussion results in a statement of important news, a decision or an agreed action, it is recorded as a summary in the minutes (along with who said it, who agreed, who took the action and by when the action will be completed).

- The time the meeting ends is also noted in the minutes.

You may tend to take minutes on a laptop so that you don't have to type them again after the meeting. It is easier if you use a template. Try some of the discussion points ahead of time, based on the agenda. Then you just need to fill in the blanks on your laptop during the meeting. Knowing a bit about the subject helps when taking minutes.

If you are a bit slow on your laptop, try writing them and type them later.

Taking minutes is all about recording a summary of the important points and decisions. But what if you don't know enough about the subject to know what is important? Try looking at the minutes of the previous meeting to prepare for what is to come, and if you're totally clueless, then speak to the meeting chairperson and ask him or her to provide you with cues as to what to record!

Remember the context

Context is important when taking minutes. If a decision was taken, for example, note down a summary of how the decision was taken, who agreed and what points were decided upon. There is no need to write chapter and verse—summarise the issues in a statement that describes the process and the outcome.

You're part of the meeting, too!

In most contemporary environments, the minute-taker is also a contributor to the meeting—so if you're taking the minutes, you don't need to stay out of the discussion. It's important that you get involved in the meeting too, if that is what is expected. However, your contribution to the discussion should not be at the expense of minute-taking. If you need time to record something, then ask for it.

Don't delay in sending the minutes

You shouldn't wait too long after the meeting to type and distribute the minutes. We tend to forget matters. Context is sometimes lost, or influenced by our own biases. The longer you wait to record the minutes, the harder it is to complete and the less accurate they become.

How To Be A Great Leader Of Team Meetings

What a feeling it is, when a team meeting goes well and your colleagues walk out with a spring in their step. Here are some tips to achieve just that!

- Do ensure that every attendee has something to contribute and something useful to take away. So make sure that you have an agenda that covers everyone's interests.

- Be inclusive—ask for their opinion. For it to be a real, all-inclusive team meeting, you must open the discussion to everyone, and the best way to do this is to ask for opinions on matters arising. And here's an important tip: never stop anyone from forming an opinion that you (or others in the group) disagree with. Everybody has a right to an opinion.

- Never leave an issue without an action! A team meeting mustn't be a place to just talk shop. If there is an issue that concerns the team, then always ensure that the meeting closes only after the issue has been allocated to someone, who will take it away to process, and a date fixed, by which the owner must report back to the team.

- **LQR—Listen-Question-Repeat:** Actively listen. Show that you're listening to your team by eye contact, the occasional nod, and a confirmation that you have listened by repeating what you have understood. Use this as an opportunity to ensure this is about what's said.

- **Keep it light:** A serious meeting can be dull; lighten the air for those involved. A little humour could lighten the mood if required (sensitively, of course).

- **Be open to challenges:** If you're just in 'broadcast-mode' then you'll see glaring eyes. People stop listening if they can't engage. If you want to effectively share information or influence, then you must allow your message to be discussed, challenged and disagreed with inside the room. If you don't, you will be challenged, passively, outside the room, and beyond your control!

- **Don't use positional power:** If you have to say something like 'Well, I am the boss, so that's what we're going to do…' then you're on a slippery slope. Using of positional power like this, is the shutting of windows. Your people will disengage and you're then on your own. It's much better to persuade. And if you can't persuade, then there is something you're not listening to.

- **Allow your weaknesses to be exposed:** Don't let ego rule.

- **Publish an agenda:** Even if it is just a list of discussion points to cover, publish an agenda. It helps in time management to have an agenda so you can stick to time and not allow one point to hijack the meeting.

- **Publish minutes:** Minutes are a record of the meeting. It gives what was discussed and what actions were agreed upon.

Don't make a meeting a long drag, one with umpteen cups of coffee and tea and biscuits. Yes, non-stop 'meetings' are one of the most energy draining and avoidable activities of the corporate world. In many organisations, a stage has been reached where the very mention of the word 'meeting' is equated with something that is boring and energy draining. Today, many managers and employees go to office just to attend meetings throughout the day without getting a chance to do any meaningful work. For example, in some organisations even the most trivial of tasks cannot be done without first calling a meeting, then a second meeting and then some more. Agreed, meetings and conference calls are necessary to run things, but instead of running things they usually end up stopping things from happening. Also, another big challenge for meeting initiators is to keep all attendees alert.

CHAIRING A MEETING

Two Common Mistakes

- Meetings are often opened by jumping straight into the 'content' (the agenda), without setting the context or enjoying a short chat among the members of the meeting.
- Meetings sometimes come to an end without clarifying the actions and the target dates, and without ensuring that they are understood.

You must remember that a meeting has people…people with worries, excitement, aspirations and frustrations… So when we ignore the people element of the group of human-beings congregating around a table, we take out the essence of getting together in the first place; you might as well hold the meeting over the telephone! A good thing is to 'humanize' our meetings.

You Could Begin

- Celebrate the success of the group or an individual, or share some other positive news. It could be as simple as talking about the weather.

- Whatever your choice of subject, talk about something positive that everyone can engage in. Try to get people smiling and a few laughs in before embarking on technical subjects. The energy levels of the group will rise.

End Of The Meeting

You may have taken notes or had someone record the minutes. The 'content' of the meeting is over, but the meeting itself is not.

Always end a meeting by summarising the content of the meeting, in most cases expressed as the agreed actions with owners. If you hadn't done so before, an expectation of the time frame for the action is discussed. It's also crucial at this point that if you suspect any action isn't clear, or hasn't been understood properly, that this is called out. A way of confirming the understanding is to ask what the output of the action is, such as a paper, a decision, etc.

Things To Do Straight-Away After A Meeting

- **Write up the minutes:** Now is the best time to check that all the minutes you wrote actually mean something to you. Leaving it to later on, when it isn't as fresh in your head, could lead to confusion and the sharing of misinformation.

- **Make sure your actions are actionable:** Use the time immediately after the meeting to make sure that there are no blockers, to your know-how, to you pursuing those actions.

- **Share the information:** Now is the time to share this information, whilst it is fresh in your head, and give co-workers the opportunity to ask questions. Often, what was discussed and agreed in a meeting affects other people, and so they should be informed.

- **Follow up:** If you need to thank the participants of the meeting for attending, do it now—it's a good opportunity to recapitulate any critical actions from the meeting. It's also a good time to remind participants if there is to be a subsequent meeting and to schedule this now in their calendars.

- **Review:** Review what worked and what didn't work. Take a moment to look back at the meeting and review what worked well and what didn't work so well. Share this with colleagues for the next meeting.

PRELIMINARY CHECKLIST
OF THE MEETINGS

- Purpose—All participants know and understand the purpose of the meeting and its desired outcomes.

- Agenda—The framework upon which the meeting rests, is organised to achieve the purpose and outcomes of the meeting.

- Participants—Those with insights or expertise, along with those who have the authority to implement the agreed upon action. They come prepared, understand their roles and are able to make contributions in an open, positive way.

- Chairperson—The chairperson guides the discussion with reference to the agenda, accommodating the varying needs and sensitivities of those present and keeping the meeting focused in the direction of the desired outcome.

- Agreed action—Before the meeting is over, the chairperson should summarise clearly what has been achieved and agreed upon.

- Follow-up—The meeting secretary records all the decisions and action points in the minutes, so that everyone can easily see what they are required to contribute to the agreed upon action at the meeting.

Self-Feedback

Look at this questionnaire. Think of what is generally true of your group meetings. If the statement expresses what is generally or usually happens at your meetings, tick 'Yes'. If it is not true of your meetings, tick 'No'. If you are uncertain, tick the 'Question mark'.

	Yes	No	?
1. A visitor would be favourably impressed by the problem-solving attitude and procedure of the group.	( )	( )	( )
2. Argumentation is at the personal level and not on 'merits'.	( )	( )	( )
3. People have a sense of accomplishment after meetings.	( )	( )	( )
4. The agenda contains items that are not appropriate or relevant for group discussion.	( )	( )	( )
5. Either before the meeting or at its beginning, any group member can easily include new items into the agenda.	( )	( )	( )
6. People come to the meetings not knowing what is to be presented or discussed.	( )	( )	( )
7. The group discusses and evaluates how decisions from previous meetings worked out.	( )	( )	( )

8. There are many problems about which people are concerned that never get on the agenda. ( ) ( ) ( )

9. When conflict arises, the group does not avoid it, but really stays with the conflict and works on it. ( ) ( ) ( )

10. Decisions are often left vague—as to what they are and who will implement them. ( ) ( ) ( )

11. The meetings begin and end on time. ( ) ( ) ( )

12. People are afraid to be openly critical or express objections. ( ) ( ) ( )

13. Disagreement is not a matter of surprise but is seen as potentially productive. ( ) ( ) ( )

14. The same few people do most of the talking during the meeting. ( ) ( ) ( )

15. The chairperson lets the group know exactly how much influence they will have on a decision. ( ) ( ) ( )

16 The same problems keep coming up at meetings. ( ) ( ) ( )

17. When the group is thinking about a problem, at least two or three different solutions are suggested before one is adopted. ( ) ( ) ( )

18. People don't seem to care about the meeting or want to get involved in it. ( ) ( ) ( )

19. The average person in the meeting feels that ideas have not been discussed. ( ) ( ) ( )

20. Solutions and decisions are in accord with the chairperson's or leader's point of view, but not necessarily with that of others. ( ) ( ) ( )

If on the odd numbers your answers are mostly 'Yes' and on the even numbers mostly 'No', your group seems to be doing well. Otherwise, there's room to improve your group's meetings.

2

Conference Meetings

Conference meeting is one in which participants in different locations are able to communicate with each other in sound and vision. Today, technology allows users in different and even distant places to hold face-to-face meetings without having to move to a single location. This includes holding routine meetings, negotiating business deals and interviewing candidates.

- **Speak or listen:** Some service providers offer the option to allow some/all participants to speak and listen, or just listen. 'Listen only' is useful for delivering broadcast updates and training courses. Not all service or service providers offer this feature.

- **Maximum number of participants:** Depending on how many concurrent participants you're likely to have, choose a service that supports your requirement. Most offer more than what you will need, but it's essential to check nonetheless.

- **Cost:** It can become very expensive for mobile users; consider services that offer a cheaper rate using a short-code number for mobile users.

- **Pay-as-you-go versus contract:** Many services are on a contract basis; you pay a subscription fee for the service and users pay a local rate to dial in. And then some services are 'free', but claw back revenue through premium rate numbers—essentially spreading the cost over the bills of participants. Regular users should choose a subscription-based plan whereas infrequent users should use a pay-as-you-go service.

- **Recording/transcription:** Some service providers offer recording and/or transcriptions so you can maintain a record of calls. This is especially useful when negotiating with suppliers or dealing with contracts.

- **Leaders:** With non-leader services, anybody can initiate and join.

- **Integration into other services:** Some services allow you to integrate into others, such as WebEx, where you can conference not only by voice, but also through a browser and share desktops. Interactive sessions using screen-sharing are very effective in demonstrating applications, video or highly-visual presentations.

- **'Vanity' numbers:** You might want your dial-in number to be unique to your brand. Some services offer this.

- **Contract length:** You may be in contract for a long term, but then again, you might not be. Consider the contract duration of the service before renewing, as you might find yourself bound to a contract you no longer might require. Short contracts, however, tend to cost more per month.

VIDEO CONFERENCING

Video conferencing has become a standard practice in many industries. New technology has made it easier than ever to connect with partners, clients and employees across the globe. It's important for businesses to effectively train their employees about video conferences as it becomes more widely used throughout the world.

Dos

- Mute your microphone whenever you're not speaking— even if you're alone in the room. Background noise can be an annoying distraction and stifle any meeting's flow.

- Be aware of your video settings. Make sure your microphone is 'On' before delivering a two-minute monologue that no one will hear.

- Make sure your room is well lit. Few things are worse than having a professional meeting while feeling like you're talking to someone in a closet. Use natural light from windows or simply turn on the overhead light in the room to brighten up the conference.

- Wear appropriate clothing. Be formal. I know it can be tempting—especially if you work from home—to wear a work shirt and sports shorts but dress as if you're meeting face to face. You may have to get up suddenly or your camera might fall. So wear clean, professional clothing for your video calls.

- Your wall art or decorations should be work appropriate and your surroundings clean. If your room is in disarray, tidy it up or use a different room. This also includes your desk! Avoid having several coffee mugs on it.

- Test your microphone before you video call, especially if it's an important meeting. Test it by video conferencing a colleague before the meeting. Nothing is worse than trying to share something critical and not being able to communicate clearly because your audio clarity and volume is poor.

- If you're in a group, a call without video, first introduce yourself before you actually begin. Consider something like 'Hi, it's Robin; I have a question.' While several programmes will notify you as to who is talking, conference line numbers will not. Therefore, be polite and introduce yourself.

- When you're talking, look into the camera instead of looking at yourself on the computer screen. It will help others on the call feel like you're 100 per cent engaged and present.

Don'ts

- Don't position your camera too low, too high or hooked to a different monitor. Weird camera angles can be very distracting during video conference calls. Make sure your camera is at eye level and on the monitor you plan to use for the conference.

- Check or read emails or peruse articles while on the video call. This also includes doing other work while on the call. It's easy for other participants to tell if you aren't focused during the video call.

It's important to remember that video conferences are essentially in-person interactions that allow businesses to communicate more effectively.

Inside Out: IP Address

- Make sure you have the IP address of the site you want to call or that the site is listed in a directory.

- Preset your camera before you start your call so that you can quickly use them during the call.

- Use the 'mute' button on the remote control when another site/person is speaking, and deactivate it when you wish to speak.

- Avoid 'double talk'; allow the other site/person to finish speaking before you speak. Double talking may cause audio feedback and echo from the audio bridge.

- Set up the equipment before the scheduled time so you have time to test the system and resolve any issues before the meeting.

Inside Out: Tips For Great Video

- Avoid wearing bright colours, all-light or all-dark clothing, or very 'busy' patterns (such as small checks or narrow stripes). Pastels and muted colours look best on the screen.

- If there are windows in the room, close the drapes or blinds. Daylight is a variable light source and can conflict with interior room lighting.

- Use natural gestures when you speak.

- When adjusting your camera, try to fill the screen as much as possible with people rather than with table, chairs, walls, lights or the floor.

Inside Out: Tips For Great Audio

- Speak in your normal voice.

- Ask the people at the other site if they can hear you.

- Have them introduce themselves so you can be sure that you can hear them.

- Mute the microphone before moving it during a meeting.

- Since the audio has a very slight delay, you may want to pause briefly for others to answer you or to make comments.

- As with any meeting, try to limit side conversations.

- Place the microphone on the table in front of the people in the meeting.

Inside Out: Tips For Showing Content

- Check that your computer has the application you need to show your documents, such as Microsoft PowerPoint, Project or Word.

- For a smoother presentation, make sure your presentation is ready to show. Test it before you start the call.

3

Stand-Up Meetings

A stand-up meeting (or 'stand-up') is a daily team meeting with the primary goal of providing a status update to the team members. It allows participants to learn about potential challenges facing the team, as well as manage issues that could take the progress off track. The term 'stand-up' comes from having participants physically stand at the meeting in order for meetings to be short.

Typically, a stand-up meeting will take ten or fifteen minutes.

Stand-ups are commonly used in 'Agile' software development methodologies, such as 'Scrum'. However, they can be effectively used in any project or even in an operational environment.

The 'meeting culture' is changing—many organisations are changing the way they have meetings. Indeed, no more rushing ones—these are signs of things to come.

You've probably been in meetings where the chair is a comfortable zone in which you can sit and listen, day-dream or completely switch off. But more and more organisations are mandating that employees stay attentive and erect.

The pace of modern organisation or businesses is demanding employees to be sharper and keener, and slouching has no place.

Demand The Stand

So if our meetings are failing to create the right momentum, we can try demanding that they be conducted in stand-up fashion. We choose a room with no central table and chairs, and we get right to it. Standing meetings have to be sharper or attendees will start shuffling from foot to foot, so we've got to be prepared to drive the meeting forward at a fast pace.

We must cut the small talk, chit-chat. We must ask direct questions and demand direct answers. We have to maintain pace. This is easier than you might think.

When you run standing meetings, the very fact of being upright helps the oxygen course through your veins faster.

You could use stand-up meetings in all sorts of projects to manage programmes and projects. These are much more effective than weekly meetings since you don't have to wait a week to share information and get a grip on issues.

There are normally three questions asked (and answered) in daily stand-up meetings.

- What did I accomplish yesterday?
- What will I do today?
- What obstacles are impeding my progress?

Stand-ups are usually held at the same time and place each working day, if logistics allow. If any team members can't attend, the meeting is normally held anyway.

Why Stand-up Meetings?

These meetings are intended to encourage better team working. The meeting itself shouldn't be the end of the discussion, but instead promote follow-up conversations.

A great benefit of the daily meeting is that issues are identified at a finer and subtler level and can be dealt with before too much time causes the issue to escalate. Contrast this to a weekly meeting where issues found on a Tuesday aren't reported until the following Monday's team meeting.

Because they are short, these meetings don't take up a lot of time and they don't feel as the longer weekly meetings. Participants have to prepare for them much less too.

Such meetings form a platform for better knowledge-sharing and awareness of responsibilities and tasks across the team. This, in turn, will lead to less email traffic between team members and having new members of the team on board in a much simpler way.

What's more, the 'energy' of a stand-up is much better and participants are sharper and more eager. It feels more like fun.

The final point is that there is no absolute rule of how to run a stand-up meeting. It's a concept which can be adapted to your needs and you should look to constantly improve and fine-tune it.

Rapid decision-making

Almost all views of the future indicate the need to cope with ever-increasing rates of change. Decision-making must therefore, become more efficient. Effective meetings are a valuable means of bringing together key people to discuss and resolve issues that could affect most people.

Disseminating information

Through meetings, a good deal of information can be effectively passed on—information which might otherwise be unclear or uninteresting and therefore unheeded—in written 'memo' form. The format of the meeting encourages two-way communication. The more involved the staff feel in the process, the more likely they are to take ownership of the information and ideas presented to them.

Internal changes

A great deal of resistance to change, stems from staff feeling that they are not being consulted over issues or long-term plans that directly concern them. Any organisation that intends to follow a new direction or adopt new policies will need to bring staff together as often as possible.

Through consultation on new policies and procedures, meetings can be a means for working through the need for change and the methods of implementation. The end result will be considerably more successful than leaving staff in the dark, uninvolved and resentful.

External changes

For an increasing number of organisations, change in their external business environment is now so rapid that the corresponding need to share information internally is vital.

This could be information about their competitors, the general economic climate, press coverage of their products and so forth.

After all, sales personnel are often better placed than senior management to gauge the changing needs of the market, via their day-to-day contact with actual customers. Meetings provide a situation where such knowledge can be passed on to key decision-makers or other departments.

Regular meetings can also put together significant information from different departments, allowing all those affected by changes or decisions to be presented with a 'total picture'. Again, this will foster increased cooperation with respect to any decisions made at the meeting.

Exchange of ideas and experience

While memos are merely able to circulate information, meetings can both encourage comments on that information and aid further development of the ideas put forward. By bringing together a number of different perspectives, meetings can produce new ideas or new ways of solving problems that may not have been considered before.

Many creative methods can be employed in a group situation to develop new approaches to long-standing problems. A useful and stimulating technique is 'brainstorming'. This generates a large number of ideas from a group of people in a short span of time, by encouraging them to contribute ideas in a spontaneous, unself-conscious way.

Developing teamwork

When staff members need to work closely together, meetings can be a means of dissipating suspicion and fear of the unknown. They can also help to overcome unhealthy rivalry.

The same is true when there have been recent changes or upheavals that have not been fully explained to staff. To gain a favourable outcome, meetings should help to develop mutual respect and understanding amongst the participants by involving them in a cooperative way.

The Task And Skills Of
The Chairperson

PLANNING FOR THE MEETING

This chapter is about meetings from the perspective of the chairperson, as most of the burden for planning and preparation will usually fall on the chairperson's shoulders. Nevertheless, each individual participant can, and should, take responsibility for the success of the meeting.

TYPES OF MEETINGS

Informative/Advisory

- both to give and receive information and thereby to keep 'in touch'
- to coordinate activities
- to record progress towards stated goals

Consultative

- resolving objections
- involving people in change or a new course of action

- simply to 'get to know' people as a means of fostering greater understanding

Problem-Solving

- to generate ideas
- to identify alternative courses of action
- to initiate that action

Decision-Taking

- to generate commitment
- to take decisions
- to share responsibility
- to initiate action

Negotiating

- to come to an agreement or contract
- to find the best solution, quite often a mutually agreeable compromise

REASONS FOR HAVING A MEETING

As chairperson, your first priority at the planning stage is to review the main purpose of the meeting—even question whether it is really necessary at all. Would other courses of action be more likely to yield the desired outcome?

Alternatives To Meetings

- **An executive decision:** Sometimes a manager has the necessary information to take a decision without any further consultation.

- **Memo, letter, fax or e-mail message:** If the objective is to pass on non-controversial information to other members of staff, then written communication may be cheaper and more effective.

- **Telephone:** Simply engaging in a few important two-way discussion over the telephone with the key individuals concerned can render a meeting superfluous.

- **Video conference:** Already a viable alternative for many organisations. Long-distance telephone contact with a video link-up can greatly reduce the need for costly travel.

Aim At A Goal

Establish others to think through, what you feel could be the most effective outcome of the issue at hand. Consider whether this is attainable in one meeting, or is simply a staging post on the way to something else.

- **Ideal outcome:** Get all the key objectives agreed upon, in terms that everyone can understand.

- **Realistic outcome:** Get the key objectives fully discussed and agreed to by everyone.

- **Fallback position:** Have a full and frank discussion about the objectives and identify any blocks to progress.

Considering these possible outcomes can be helpful in two ways. First, it focuses attention on the ultimate objectives of the meeting, on how everyone will benefit as a result. In addition, it will pinpoint the options that are available and give you a clear view of what you want to achieve.

PLANNING

Who Should Attend?

At this stage, you should be able to assess who will need to attend and, more importantly, who will not need to attend. This prevents staff from wasting their time attending a meeting for no apparent purpose, which is frustrating for everyone.

At regular, routine meetings attendance is rarely an issue. At other meetings, there may be scope for bringing in outside influences, experts for instance, who can enliven the meeting by offering new perspectives or sound well-informed advice.

It may also prove helpful to introduce 'disinterested parties' who can be seen, by all sides, to give an impartial view. Such people can act as useful catalysts in otherwise difficult negotiations.

In general terms, the following people need to be included.

- Those with information to give at the meeting
- Those who will gather useful information from the meeting
- Those with expertise to contribute to the meeting
- Those who for the sake of office protocol, need to be included
- Those who may be able to provide a balance in areas of instability or conflict

- Those who are empowered to implement any actions agreed upon

Setting The Agenda

This is a crucial task for the chairperson, as it defines the boundaries of the discussion that will ensue in the course of the meeting. In effect, whoever controls the agenda, controls the meeting.

The agenda has many functions.

- It can communicate certain expectations to everyone involved, well in advance.

- Later, it will act as a script or mechanism, via which the chairperson can steer the meeting.

- Ultimately, it will also serve as a standard or measure of success.

A carefully planned agenda is the most valuable tool for keeping the group's mind focused on achieving the desired outcome. In effect, it is a 'map' of the meeting that everyone can refer to. Even for short meetings of two or three people, the very act of thinking through and developing an agenda can lead to a structure that will focus on the outcomes that all those involved really want.

CREATING AN EFFECTIVE AGENDA

Preparing An Agenda

- Consider carefully, who should attend.
- Cover a few major points or issues which have a common thread.

- Structure the agenda carefully, but loosely, to allow scope for discussion.
- Try not to focus on problems, but to look at the opportunities for improvement they represent—stay positive.
- Be specific about time allocated to each issue or topic (e.g. use of washroom—five minutes), as this prevents the meeting from becoming bogged down in detail over relatively minor issues and gives some indication as to the relevant importance of each subject in the overall discussion.

When you come to sequence your agenda, you should also consider the following.

- A logical order
- Routine items
- Any special factors in this particular meeting
- Any difficult or contentious items
- A balance between urgent and important topics

For a formal meeting, the following items should be on the agenda in terms of procedure.

- Title, date, time and place of the meeting
- Apologies for absence
- Minutes of the previous meeting
- Matters arising from the previous meeting
- Other items to be discussed and decided
- Any other business
- Date, time and place for the next meeting

Before The Meeting

After the date, time and location of the meeting have been decided, and the agenda set, there is still much preparation to be done.

Planning For People

As chairperson, an important part of your preparation involves thinking through the proposed meeting long before it takes place. In other words, exploring all the possibilities, and understanding and identifying possible sticky points and thus being able to pre-empt them.

By considering the probable needs, wants and motivations of the participants, you will be able to estimate the likely course of the meeting and can approach it more comprehensively.

Questions to help your preparation

- Who will be at the meeting?
- What are they particularly concerned about, or interested in?
- What are their aims, aspirations and assumptions about the meeting—particularly where contentious issues are likely to arise?
- How do you envisage reconciling these individual aims, aspirations and assumptions into a coherent whole?
- Who has the authority to get things done?
- What are your priorities for achieving the desired

outcomes—and what particular issues might get in the way of you achieving them?

- How can you ensure that all those participating prepare effectively for the meeting?

Pre-meeting Papers And Notifying People

Obviously, as chairperson, you must familiarise yourself with any meeting papers or relevant information sent out with the agenda. Less obviously, but equally importantly, you must encourage everyone participating in the meeting to do their 'homework'.

One way of doing this is to get into the habit of starting the meeting with the clear assumption that everyone is properly prepared. Participants will quickly understand that valuable time will not be devoted to debating minor details of pre-meeting papers—or demotivating those who have prepared diligently by reiterating information for those who haven't!

Preparation Of A Checklist

So, when you prepare for a meeting, make sure you have allowed time for the following.

- Doing your own 'homework' on the agenda

- Notifying all participants in good time

- Making sure that all who are invited can attend

- Making sure the meeting room is ready

- Making sure participants have enough time to meet any special technical needs for visual aids, presentations, etc.

Meeting In Process

At any kind of meeting, which takes place at regular intervals, certain recognisable patterns of behaviour will become apparent to the chairperson. In order to develop real skills in managing meetings, it is necessary to become attuned to these patterns, as they will exert a good deal of influence over group behaviour and thinking.

UNDERSTANDING GROUPS

The most powerful interests in any meeting—far more powerful than the purported objectives of the meeting itself—are the basic human needs of the participants. These include:

- economic well-being,
- a sense of belonging,
- the need for recognition, and
- control of one's own life.

These needs will be expressed at nearly every point in a meeting, whether or not participants voice them directly. By recognising such motivating factors and appealing to people's interests anyone can potentially support, or alternately undermine, the stated agenda. The chairperson cannot afford to ignore any such factors as they concern the way in which groups come together, and then develop around the common perception of a given task.

Group Behaviour

A greater appreciation of the behaviour of groups helps both the chairperson and individual participants to understand what is really going on at the meeting. As we all know, what people say is not necessarily what they mean—how they say it and why they say it, is often far more significant.

This can be beneficial to the chairperson, in particular.

- Certain phases of group development can be analysed and predicted.
- Many of the sources of futile conflict can be anticipated and pre-empted.

Acceptance And Integration

To a greater or lesser extent, all people look for some identity within a group and a sense of belonging. This applies not only to work situations but also to our roles within a family or social circle.

Anyone entering an established group will be particularly aware of his or her own need for acceptance—hence new arrivals will tend to conform more to existing norms of behaviour within the group, rather than immediately expressing their individuality.

Chairperson's Approach

If a new chairperson approaches the meeting determined to impose his views as a palpable show of strength—'starting as they mean to go on'—he is likely to provoke both resentment and resistance.

Newly Established Groups

Where a group is newly established, things tend to develop in a different way. Theoretically, all participants will be looking to gain acceptance or establish some form of group identity—the starting point, at least, will be the same for everyone. Nevertheless, as different participants engage themselves with varying degrees of effort or effectiveness, some may find themselves marginalised, while others are more firmly entrenched.

A part of the chairperson's role is to restore some of the balance by drawing members back from the fringes of the group, identifying them and encouraging their involvement.

Communication Within The Group

Meetings have suffered through the assumption that the participants only need information about the matter in hand, rather than about each other. For people to be able to work effectively together, it is important that they should be allowed to establish as many areas of common ground as possible. Even social backgrounds or shared interests help to generate understanding.

A meeting will particularly benefit from participants' knowledge of their colleagues' experience or areas of expertise—information that may help foster mutual respect and encourage a more willing acceptance of other people's input.

With effective communication and information sharing, members of a meeting can build stronger relationships, ultimately developing the confidence to share more of their real thoughts and ideas.

Group Objectives

An individual participant's objectives provide the sense of purpose which guides their efforts. Group objectives, however, are often more difficult to clarify.

Participants will often have apparently conflicting objectives, or stated group objectives, which may be little more than a mask for some 'hidden agenda'. Equally, chairpersons may have their own objectives which they seek to impose on the participants.

Uncertainty surrounding objectives, or conflict between them, will have a disastrous effect on the productivity of the meeting. It is vital that everyone, particularly the chairperson, is able to identify and agree on suitable objectives. Without this, the meeting will degenerate into a demotivating free-for-all, lacking any cooperation or overall commitment.

Group Control

Realistically, any meeting will need some form of control for its objectives to be achieved. The chairperson should ensure that everyone is given a chance to contribute.

However, methods of control are likely to inhibit the progress of a meeting if they are either over-complicated or inflexible.

- Over-complicated—The structure for making proposals or initiating action is so convoluted that sound creative ideas are lost in the process. The ideas that do get through are more likely to come from the less imaginative members of the meeting, who are more suited to mastering its structures than tackling the matter in hand.

- Inflexible—This will stifle individual input and more or less make redundant the participative framework that a meeting provides. Those members with the most to offer the meeting—in terms of creative problem-solving, for instance—are likely to react against it and be demotivated by it.

Another counter-productive effect of both these methods is to allow participants to shift responsibility for action on to the organiser or chairperson.

Ultimately, if the structure is appropriate to the meeting's aims and content, and clearly understood and accepted by the participants, it will lead to effective group working and an appropriate distribution of tasks and authority.

Group Development

Consider the following factors.

- What is the level of acceptance in the group?

- How far are individual needs met?

- What can be done to meet these needs further?

In addition, the chairperson should constantly monitor his or her own meeting group's behaviour for signs of needs met or unfulfilled.

Meeting group's needs

Although to meet all the group's needs will often be impossible to achieve on a practical level, meeting them as far as you can will promote constructive group behaviour and lead to further development.

A well-integrated group will be able to tackle the main task more efficiently and successfully than a collection of self-serving individuals pulling in all directions as an integrated group. Each individual member will actually be able to realise more of his or her own potential by a suitably concerted effort.

Group's norms

The relative success or failure of a meeting depends almost completely on the interaction between the participants. Like any group of people, they will typically develop, in four stages—*Forming, Storming, Norming* and *Performing*.

- **Forming:** The initial coming together of a new group of people and the testing of position and influence.

- **Storming:** The process of disagreeing on things such as values, methods or simply what the main task is. It is preferable to bring these differences to the surface, so that they can be confronted and resolved, rather than leave them to fester and recur later.

- **Norming:** This is what happens once the members of a group have established workable rules to which the majority subscribe. The norms, standards or expectations which people demand of one another can vary a great deal from one group to another. Even a group that has never met before will set norms for itself quite quickly.

- **Performing:** This is the last phase—the phase of group development. Each group member should be operating to the best of their ability with rules and agreed methods for, towards the overall objectives that the group has set for itself.

TASK AND PROCESS

Task behaviours emphasise the content of the work and process behaviours, and on how people relate to one another and work together.

Examples of task behaviour:

- **Initiating:** Suggesting ideas or putting forward new definitions of the problem.

- **Building:** Seeking to develop or extend a proposal which has been made by someone else.

- **Gate-keeping:** Making sure every member of the meeting is able to contribute.

- **Expressing feelings:** Summarising the way the meeting is progressing and the reactions of individuals.

SEQUENCE OF DECISION-MAKING

Decisions normally need to be taken before the end of each meeting, with a view to their subsequently being implemented. The chairperson's role involves steering the discussion towards a point at which suitable action can be agreed upon. At the same time, encouraging the maximum possible contribution from all those present is great.

- Seek agreement on the basic issues or problems to be discussed.

- Define them for everyone at the meeting, but avoid presenting such problems as if they are passive ones. The problems should be portrayed as active, encouraging people's involvement.

- Separate problems into a number of categories and decide the sequence of discussing them.

- Going through each element, in turn, will prevent you from being defeated by the scale of the overall problem.

- Put forward the facts about the newly defined problem. Be careful to distinguish between accepted 'data' (which is not to be challenged in any way) and judgements or opinions (generally a reflection of people's preferences and prejudices).

- Now, allow the participants to discuss their interpretation of the basic data.

- Now, move on to considering alternate courses of action. These arise from the participants' own interpretations of the problem.

- Decide on different courses of action—Participants' own criteria for taking a decision and what the potential advantages and disadvantages might be.

- Ensure that someone is made responsible for taking follow-up action on the decision.

- The name of the speaker should be recorded in the minutes. The results of their actions can then form the basis for any further meetings on the subject.

Tasks Of The Chairperson

These can be split into six categories.

- Getting the meeting under way.

- Guiding the meeting on, through each successive stage by way of the agenda.
- Summarising each stage before moving on — thereby unequivocally establishing what has been the agreed course of action.
- Ensuring a written record is kept of all mutual decisions and agreed action — this can then be referred back to as an aid to later meetings.
- Guiding the participants away from areas of conflict.
- Ensuring that all participants have the opportunity to contribute to the meeting.

APPROACHING THE MEETING

The First Act

The chairperson must first open the meeting in an appropriate way. As ever, first impressions are disproportionately important! The way that you, as chairperson, start the meeting will probably have an enormous impact on how your input will be received and how people will react to you during the course of the meeting.

It is only by considering the individual needs, wants and motivations of the other participants that you will be able to tailor your approach to the demands of the situation.

Presentation

Remember, what you actually say is only a part of the impression you give to others. Your non-verbal behaviour will communicate with your tone of voice, facial expressions and general body language. If your mood is cheerful and optimistic, you will send a positive signal to them. Conversely, should you seem pessimistic or generally unenthusiastic, this is bound to have a demotivating effect on the meeting.

Chairperson's Preparation

Well before the meeting, you should give careful consideration to the actual process that is to take place—forewarned is forearmed! Obviously, the clearer an idea you have of the desired outcome, the better able you will be to respond during the meeting.

While preparing, take the following into consideration.

- What do you want to have achieved by the end of the meeting?

- Who will be attending?

- What do they want to have achieved by the end of the meeting?

- What are their roles in relation to you?

- What kind of prejudices or preconceptions do they bring with them and how might these affect their role at the meeting?

- What shared ideas or philosophies do you all have that could form a common ground in the meeting?

- What could you say or do to emphasise these areas of common ground particularly at the outset of the meeting?

All these questions will guide you to a greater understanding of the participants and their role. This can also help you identify areas, which you are not fully aware of or where you require greater knowledge or understanding.

From the outset, you not only need to get the attention of the participants, but also make them all feel that they can contribute. Wit and humour may help, if you feel comfortable with that style, although a forced jocular style is more likely to arouse suspicion than anything else.

Even if you feel unable to joke convincingly to put people at their ease, it is good practice to plan a remark that could 'break the ice' in some way and hopefully point to some sort of common bond. This helps the participants to relate to you in a way they might not have anticipated before the meeting.

In your entire approach, apparent confidence is of key importance. As chairperson, you should look and sound as though you expect the meeting to achieve its objectives easily—sometimes quite a challenge!

ESTABLISH OBJECTIVES

It important that, at the outset, you clearly state the main purpose of the meeting and give some idea of its intended structure. Provide an overview of the subject or issues involved and introduce any relevant experts or specialists, who have been brought in to participate.

These early remarks should be made as clear as possible to set the meeting off in the right direction. You may find it useful to write them down and rehearse them a few times, so that you will be able to put them across effectively at the actual meeting.

Establish Timescales

At the outset, establish the timescale of the meeting and the time allocated to each area of discussion. State when you expect the meeting to finish. This prevents participants from assuming that the discussion is an open-ended one, giving them free rein to digress into areas of self-interest.

Consider Others

It is important that you develop a good understanding of the participants and their interests. Appealing to these interests may, at some point, mean ending the meeting as soon as possible! Even this is legitimate, if it means that the participants are encouraged to make the best use of the time there is.

You should be able to communicate on a level that they will readily understand—saying what needs to be said and avoiding areas of needless conflict.

Stimulate Discussion

Present items simply and concisely in a firm, confident manner. Aim to introduce a topic in such a way that you stimulate discussion from a number of perspectives. Where someone appears reticent or disinclined to offer an opinion, try to build their confidence and draw them into the discussion: 'Well, Michael, what's your perspective on this?'

Limit Conflict

When dealing with contentious issues, where there is likely

to be conflict between participants, try to limit the debate by suggesting boundaries to what is to be discussed.

Expect The Unexpected

Along with all the things that you, as chairperson, can plan ahead for are those circumstances which are out of your control. Hence you will need to take into account both late arrivals and early departures, minimising any detrimental effect they may have on the flow of the meeting.

STRUCTURE THE MEETING

It is your job, as chairperson, to structure the meeting — making the best use of the time available, to obtain the desired outcome. Different types of meetings will require different styles and methods of control.

Even between one item on an agenda and another, you may be required to modify your approach to an appreciable extent, balancing the need to allow free-flowing discussion within the constraints of time. While defining strict limits as to who speaks, how they speak and for how long; you must also create the opportunity for active contributions from all present.

Use Background Information

For each item on the agenda, you should provide background information—as to previously agreed courses of action—which provides both context and perspective for discussion of the current situation. This will give participants a better idea of what is required and could prevent duplication of efforts by highlighting already explored avenues.

Encourage Controlled Discussion

The next step is to stimulate discussion from several points of view. This is obviously important, as the reason for having a meeting, rather than issuing a directive or memo, is to encourage discussion from a variety of perspectives. All the while, however, you must keep things within the structure of the agenda—in order to prevent the meeting from degenerating into a personal confrontation.

The same control must apply to the time allowed for each topic. Although you need to give the participants a certain amount of time to explore the issues involved, if they are left for too long, they will lose focus, perhaps become bored, and drift into inconsequential side issues.

SUMMARISING

This is an important skill for the chairperson to acquire. It can be used for a number of purposes at different stages of the meeting to:

- signal to a participant that they have 'had their say' and that it may be time to allow another member of the meeting to speak.

- signal the end of one phase of the discussion or form the basis of another.

- bring together the disparate strands of the discussion, particularly where this has rambled on for some time and you need to draw together a series of complicated arguments.

- gauge the degree of real agreement that exists over a particular decision.

- clarify exactly what has been agreed.

- confirm agreed action.

- help the meeting secretary write accurate, and therefore useful, minutes.

CONTROL

The chairperson needs to strike a fine balance between two quite different aspects of control: procedural control and process control.

Procedural Control

- Stick to the agenda

- Keep to the time

- Keep the discussion on the issue at hand

- Make decisions

- Agree to actions

These are all good, solid requirements that might lead you to believe that a chairperson must rule with the proverbial 'iron rod'. Nevertheless, the following should also be borne in mind.

Process Control

At the same time as fulfilling those rather stringent requirements, the chairperson must also ensure that everyone present has an opportunity to air his or her views. For this to happen the chairperson must:

- facilitate discussion.

- involve all participants.
- encourage different views and perspectives.
- allow extensive debate on those items that warrant it.
- encourage creativity.

Remember, it is precisely because there is a framework and a degree of 'discipline' that everyone will have a chance to contribute.

FACILITATING DISCUSSION

The skills involved in facilitating discussion can be broken down and learnt in these ways.

Listening

This means not only the verbal content, what someone actually says at a meeting, but also the range of non-verbal messages that are communicated at the same time, including:

- the actual feeling behind the message,
- the tone and pitch of the voice, and
- the things that aren't said.

Posture And Facial Expressions

Listening in this way can be a demanding process. To do it successfully, you will need to concentrate hard and pay a good deal of attention to whoever is speaking.

Dealing With Difficult Participants

In any group of people, there are bound to be a few that you, as chairperson, find difficult to control in an appropriate way.

- The person who talks too much.
- The person who wants an immediate decision on everything.
- The person who makes dogmatic statements.
- The person who takes up personal 'duels' with other people.
- The person who is inattentive, whispering incessantly, or simply not listening.

In dealing with such participants, you should depersonalise the issue away from them, usually with questions which refer the problem back to group opinion.

- 'Does the group feel we are making progress?'
- 'Do you think your approach will really help us to reach a solution?'

Quite often you can bring the discussion back into focus by merely restarting the topic. At other times, a pause in proceedings may be desirable to allow the airing of feelings, or for exploratory discussion. Allowing participants to get certain things out of their system may sometimes be the only way for the meeting to progress.

DIFFICULT SITUATIONS

If someone extends the discussion beyond the topic as outlined by the chairperson—The chairperson should intervene and explain that the discussion is drifting away from the matter at hand.

Someone becomes muddled and confused—The chairperson must be supportive, coaxing the participant to restate the point more explicitly.

Someone rambles on at great length—The chairperson must intervene to save the meeting's valuable time. Nevertheless, this should be done in a sensitive and supportive way.

Someone habitually makes vague suggestions—The chairperson must clarify these suggestions before allowing the discussion to proceed.

Someone habitually interrupts other participants while they are speaking—This may be acceptable if the speaker is being corrected on a factual error. Similarly, a humorous interjection may be useful in keeping the discussion on friendly, cooperative terms. If not, then the chairperson must keep a control on who speaks and when.

Someone persists in chatting with the person sitting next to him/her—The chairperson needs to draw attention to the matter in hand and encourage everyone to pay attention. A direct question can be effective in keeping people listening actively.

General Guidelines

As chairperson, your skills in dealing with awkward people—or the resultant awkward situations—are important in adequately fulfilling that role. Here are a few helpful guidelines.

- Accept people as they are.

- Stay in the present, don't dwell on the past.

- Treat people individually—taking into account their personality—in order to treat them equally.

- Trust others, even if you feel there is a risk in doing so.

- Do not rely on constant approval—achieving popularity is not the primary objective!

Improving Participation

So far an assumption has been made that the role of the chairperson is to control the meeting, in a positive and constructive fashion. A more informal style of control is required, when the meeting's purpose is to solve a problem or learn something new. Here, participants should be enabled to take on more responsibility for the meeting's outcome by sharing the role of chairperson or facilitator.

CHAIRPERSON AS FACILITATOR

Facilitator's Role

The term 'facilitator' is used for the person who enables individuals in a group or meeting to learn and develop their potential by focusing on the ways in which they interact with each other.

In order to run a more participative meeting, the chairperson has to use many of the skills of the facilitator. For example, conflict is always with us—instead of smoothing over, ignoring or compromising in the face of it, the meeting can directly confront conflict. Its resolution will result in increased commitment to working together by keeping everybody involved.

Open Communication

For a team meeting to be successful, the participants must discuss and criticise each other's suggestions without feeling threatened. They need to cultivate the skill of open communication. When holding a problem-solving meeting with your subordinates, it is not advisable to begin by stating your own preferences. This will discourage your team from expressing their views.

A better strategy is first to find out whether the team shares your understanding of the problem. Once this has been established, the facilitator can both invite and encourage their ideas and solutions.

Competitiveness and individualism initially appear threats to cooperation and teamworking, but the manner in which these instincts are channelled and directed will determine their influence, be it positive or negative. There must be a foundation of mutual trust and respect between participants before participative processes can have the desired effect.

Skills Of The Facilitator

- Create a climate of support and openness within the group—Participants feel confident enough to contribute fully and freely to the meeting.

- Encourage participants to express their feelings and contribute their ideas—Help those present to feel they belong to the team. Involvement in discussion, contribution of ideas and arriving at group decisions generate a feeling of ownership and commitment to those decisions on the part of the participant. Ideally, the end result should be greater than the sum of the participants! This concept (put simply 2 + 2 = 5) is known as 'synergy'.

- Encourage active participation and share the leadership role—Over a period of time, team members can be led by a skilful facilitator to appreciate that each person has some expertise they can contribute to the meeting and to give them the opportunity to do so.

EFFECTIVE GROUPS

Research into group behaviour has shown that complete control and manipulation of a group by a so-called expert is very difficult and largely self-defeating. A well-organised and well-integrated group can be very successful in decision making, organising and functioning responsibly.

The results of this research show that the characteristics of an effective group, as opposed to an ineffective group, are:

Improving participation

Characteristic	Effective Group	Ineffective Group
Atmosphere	Informal, relaxed; all members involved and interested	Formal, tense; undercurrents of indifference
Discussions	Everyone contributes with relevance to task	Dominated by a few; is often irrelevant
Objectives	Formulated by all members—understood and accepted	Not clearly defined; individuals have private aims

Characteristic	Effective Group	Ineffective Group
Listening	Everyone prepared to listen; members put forward their own views	Poor; often responding to irrelevant matters
Disagreements	Careful attempts at resolution	Suppressed or open conflict; aggressive sub-group
Decisions	General consensus but individuals free to disagree	No systematic discussion of method
Criticism	Seen as constructive; welcomed	Destructive
Feelings	People free to express their feelings	Kept hidden under the surface
Actions	Clear and understood	Not clearly defined
Chairperson	Leadership role shifts to appropriate person	Dominates group
Review process	Frequent review	Not done

DECISION-MAKING BY CONSENSUS

Creative Role For The Facilitator

Consensus is the process of reaching an agreement on any subject under discussion without taking a vote—achieving it can certainly be quite a challenge for all those involved. Nevertheless, it represents an important process for drawing participants into a cooperative approach to problem-solving.

A fundamental requirement is for participants to view differences of opinion as being helpful, rather than destructive—a means of establishing areas of difficulty with a view to overcoming them.

Establishing Resources Or Expertise

The facilitator must look closely at the requirements of the task at hand and ensure that everyone is clear on the overall objectives. Anyone within the meeting who has the relevant expertise or knowledge should be identified and utilised. The facilitator can establish who they might be by asking simple, open-ended questions.

- 'Does anyone here have any special knowledge of this problem?'

- 'Have any of you done this sort of thing before?'

This process of acknowledging and involving those with relevant expertise serves two purposes. First, it is obviously useful in achieving an optimum resolution of the issues involved. Second, it uses people's skills in a constructive and participative way—areas of leadership with those who obviously have most to contribute. Possible conflict about who is the most empowered to recommend solution is avoided as people's strengths and expertise will have already been acknowledged.

The facilitator must also establish a baseline of knowledge, assumption and understanding about the task. The easiest way to do this is, to ask questions once again. Any technical terms or jargon need to be clarified so that all the participants will be able to make a contribution in their own terms.

Avoiding Or Resolving Conflicts

Areas of possible conflict should be identified by the facilitator, who should attempt to draw them out into the open and resolve them. Then, at least, the participants involved will feel that they have had a fair hearing with their points of view understood—if not supported—by their colleagues. This approach aims to remove any feelings of resentment or anger that may affect participants' contribution to the meeting.

Facilitator's Checklist

For the meeting to be effective, it is important for the facilitator to preserve the flexibility of the procedure—even monitoring their own role to ensure that they are influencing rather than contributing. The facilitator must, therefore, keep the following in mind.

- Is the task understood?

- Are expertise and resources identified and shared?

- Are assumptions and knowledge commonly shared?

- Is a cooperative atmosphere established?

- Have everyone's views been expressed and understood?

- Is there consensus at each successive stage?

- Has any undue influence on the facilitator's part been minimised?

NEGOTIATED AGENDA

The following guidelines represent a fairly radical rethink of some of the traditional meeting processes. In practise, however, they have proved most effective in a number of settings.

- The agenda is constructed at the outset of the meeting. Participants may add items if they can justify their relevance to the rest of the meeting.

- A separate facilitator is chosen by the meeting for each agenda item.

- Minutes are written as the meeting progresses and recorded, on a flipchart for instance, for all to refer to.

- Each item on the agenda is 'owned' by one of the participants, hence he or she will usually become the facilitator for that topic.

- The purpose of any agenda item is explicit—example information-giving or problem-solving—and must be justified by the participant who suggested it.

- The time allotted to each agenda is preset, so participants can establish the degree of urgency relevant to particular areas.

At the heart of this meeting process is the conscious use of time, the setting of priorities and the establishing of clearly defined roles at the meeting. In one work situation where these procedures have been introduced, the time spent in routine meetings has dropped by a third.

ONE-GOAL APPROACH

This approach is most useful if the meeting is primarily to increase the skills of the participants. The term 'learning community' has been used to sum up both the intention and the method. It is especially useful where the meeting is one where the objective is a sharing of ideas or complementary skills.

ONE—establishing the role of participants

Offers—to contribute to the meeting effectively

Needs—from the meeting

End result—that is expected by the end of the meeting

The facilitator opens the meeting by explaining that the agenda is to be negotiated and agreed to by the participants. Each of them is invited to introduce themselves and outline their experiences, stating in simple terms:

- what they can **offer** or contribute to the meeting,

- what they specifically **need** from the meeting, and

- what particular **end result** they are looking for.

The facilitator can then write these ideas, perhaps on a flipchart, so that all the participants have a clear overview of each other's approach to the meeting.

GOA…L — Negotiating the agenda

Get

Others'

Agreement

This involves establishing the agenda by mutual consent, agreeing upon the timing as well as the sequence of the discussion topics or issues. The facilitator should carefully observe participants' non-verbal reactions to assess where areas of disagreement may arise.

Limit Discussion

Having guided the participants to the agreement on the agenda and the desired end results, the facilitator can now limit the discussion to the areas to which everyone is able to contribute. Where participants drift away from the main points, the facilitator will be able to draw them back to the point with the implied consent of all concerned. This process is valuable in focusing everyone's attention on the matters at hand.

5

Rules Of Order

Everyone who chairs a formal meeting should be familiar with the basic concepts of Roberts' *Rules of Order* in an ideal situation—where there is a good chairperson and effective contributions from participants. It is still advisable to know them, however, as there are certain circumstances where they can be extremely useful.

- For certain contentious items for short periods
- At the meetings of many civic and charitable organisations, which are run along strict parliamentary lines

These are the key points of a formal procedure.

- Any motion should be proposed and seconded before discussion of the issue starts. (This is to ensure that the subject deserves discussion.)
- The chairperson should restate the motion after it has been proposed so it is clear that it has been ruled in order. (This also helps the chairperson to control the meeting.)
- Only one main motion (one that brings an action before the group) can be considered at a time.
- The main motion can be changed or disposed of by a subsidiary motion. For example: 'I move that

the minutes be amended to delete paragraph 5.' The subsidiary motion must be discussed and voted on, although it cannot be made unless the main motion is already under consideration, that is, discussion of it has already begun.

- A privilege motion is one that calls for immediate action of the whole meeting. For example, 'I move that we recess.' It must be considered before any other motion and is not debatable.

- A motion to reconsider a previous vote must be made by someone on the winning side.

- When someone 'calls for the previous question', it is only a suggestion to end the discussion and vote. If a single person objects, you must keep the discussion going. If someone 'moves the previous question' and there is a second, you must vote on whether or not to end the debate. If the motion fails, the discussion continues.

- As a general rule, do not attempt to draft any resolution that affects the constitution or conduct of the organisation, longer than a single sentence, in a formal meeting. Refer it to a committee or back to staff.

Running Meetings With Rules Of Order

A meeting wouldn't be a meeting without some general rules of procedure and decorum.

Getting to speak

When you have something to say, you have to be recognised by the chairperson. According to the *Rules of Order*, this is done by standing up and addressing the chairperson. Now, this may be a bit too formal for many occasions and, admittedly, a few people shouting 'Mr President' every few minutes gets really annoying.

As a common courtesy, you should never seek recognition while someone else is talking. There's nothing more frustrating than trying to get a point across while a dozen people have their hands in the air and are trying so hard to get the chairperson's attention that they are not paying attention to anything being said. Be polite and wait until they are finished.

There are a few instances when it is acceptable to interrupt someone or speak without gaining recognition by the chairperson, such as when making a point of order or a point of information.

According to the rules, each member can only speak twice on any given topic.

Additionally, the chairperson is obliged to try and alternate recognising those who are for and against the motion being discussed. For example, if someone just spoke against a motion, the chairperson would say something like: 'Is there anyone who wishes to speak in favour of the motion?' and then recognise someone.

Speaking

After you've been recognised, you may speak. It's best to start by addressing the chairperson, but again this may be a bit formal for chapter meetings. Always address your comments to the chairperson, even if they involve another member. This keeps the debate from becoming personal. When referring to other members, use their title and not their name. Using someone's first name implies a level of friendship that may not be appropriate when some of the members present may not know each other very well.

You may speak only on the merits of the topic. Anything off the topic is out of order, and you can be made to stop talking if someone points it out.

You may speak only for a certain length of time on any given topic. Rules allow for ten minutes, the standing rules of convention allow for two minutes.

Situations

This is a quick guide listing common situations.

- I want to change the wording of the motion we are discussing.

- Move to amend the motion and state your change specifically.

- You must be recognised by the chairperson.

- Requires a second.

- Is debatable.

- Requires a two-thirds to pass.

- I want to end the discussion and have the vote.

- Move to the previous question. Remember, when you are voting on the previous question you are voting only on whether or not to end discussion on the motion, not on the motion itself.

- I think the discussion should continue, but I don't want it to go on all day.

- Move to limit debate and state specifically how you want to limit it.

- I want the chairperson to enforce rules about time limits and the number of times people are allowed to speak.

- Make a point of order and then point out the rules being violated. The chairperson is then obliged to enforce the rules.

- The chair has been enforcing rules about time limits and the number of times people are allowed to speak, but I really think we need to discuss this more.

Point Of Order

This is used to point out when something is against the rules, which can be anything from someone talking too long to a vote being done improperly. If something is out of order, all you have to do is get the chairperson's attention by saying 'point of order', and then describe how the rules are being broken. Then, the chairperson has to enforce the rule you pointed out.

Point Of Information

There are two basic types of this.

- The first is when you want to ask a question of the maker of a motion or someone who has already spoken. To do this, just wait until no one else is speaking and then get the chairperson's attention by saying 'Point of Information' and then ask for permission to ask a question. The chairperson can then decide whether or not to allow you to ask the question.

- The second type of point of information is the parliamentary inquiry. You can make one of these when you are unsure of how to properly do something, or are confused as to what is going on and want some clarification. Again, when no one is speaking, you can get the chairperson's attention by saying 'Point of Information,' say you have a parliamentary inquiry, and then ask the chairperson your question. When you make a parliamentary inquiry, the chairperson does not have the right to decide whether or not to allow you to ask the question—he has to answer it.

Voting: Different Types Of Votes

Voice vote

The most common type of voting is when the chairperson says 'Those in favour of the motion, say "Aye".' All members in support of the motion call out 'aye'. Next, the chairperson says, 'Those opposed, say "No",' after which opponents call out "No". If there is a clear majority, the chairperson announces the result. If there is not a clear majority, a member may call for the vote to be retaken by calling out 'Division'.

Hand vote

A hand vote works the same as a voice vote, where the chairperson first calls for those in favour to raise their hands. Without counting, they then call for those opposed to raise their hands. If a majority is seen, the chairperson will announce the result. Again, a member may call 'Division' if they believe there was not a clear majority. In addition, a member may ask that the vote be counted. The chairperson then retakes the vote in the same way but counts the votes for and against the motion.

Counted vote

This is simply the counted version of the hand vote. Some groups may choose to skip the uncounted hand vote since it really does little more than the voice vote.

Roll call vote

It is not uncommon to see the roll call vote at a convention, but it typically does not happen during chapter meetings. If you still want to know what it is, read on. A roll call vote is literally what you think it would be. The chairperson reads the names of each voting member, and after hearing their name, the member calls out 'Yes' (or 'Aye') or 'No'. This may be a bit intense for chapter meetings, where votes may be more personal than convention voting, where one person's vote represents a group of people.

Secret ballot

This is the one type of vote where each member's vote choice is not known to anyone else. This is used for elections, but it may also be used for regular motions, especially for more sensitive topics. This is also the most paper-traceable vote and the final destination if 'Division' is repeatedly called for. A ballot vote may be called for when the original motion is initially about to be voted upon.

6

One-On-One Meetings

The one-on-one meeting is a proven management technique. This communication is a key to business success because it resolves issues and generates new ideas. One-on-one meetings allow employees to express their thoughts and ideas, while they aid managers in overseeing-employees' productivity and career development. The one-on-one meeting is not 'just another meeting'. This provides insights into agendas and questions.

The first thing you need to do is make your one-on-one meeting a priority. One has to schedule a recurring calendar event each week to ensure the appropriate time is set aside.

Establish The Right One-On-One Meeting Agenda

One must start each meeting with a clear agenda. Some managers like to create a structured agenda; other managers prefer to have each employee create the agenda. The key here is consistency–setting a mutually agreeable agenda allows the participants to show up prepared and with aligned expectations.

Prepare So You Can Look Forward, Not Backwards

The key to success is thoughtful preparation. Both must know everything that's been accomplished, all plans and any areas of friction. Such a foundation of understanding allows you to spend the bulk of your time looking to the future, brainstorming, creating action items and connecting personally.

Make It A Bilateral, Personal Conversation

One must certainly make sure that a one-on-one meeting is not one-sided. There is a need for a fluid conversation, with a paradigm of give and take. These meetings ought to be a forum to collectively discuss not only business, but generally how the team is doing. Discuss employee morale; ensure your team members are comfortable with their career and personal development.

Keep The Focus At The Objective Level

Use your one-on-one time to check objective progress. Effective managers are strong sounding boards and strategic thinkers—use that skill set to help your employees navigate pitfalls and address challenges in their pursuit of objective success. While you don't need to connect at the task level during the meeting, do focus on the most important upcoming plans and recent accomplishments related to a person's objectives. This will allow you to be specific in your feedback without micro-managing.

Get Started

Consider having your one-on-one meeting outside or out of the office—the change of venue can contribute to a more relaxed session. Avoid discussing other employees' work during your time together, unless it's specifically applicable to the conversation. Appreciate each employee's need for career development. Ask them what they like and don't like about their role. Explore areas of professional interest.

Don't forget to save a portion of each one-on-one for open commentary and questions. Your employee needs to be able to ask questions and give you candid feedback.

Note:

- *Shift your mindset:* See these meetings as development opportunities, not just opportunities to 'check in'. Indeed, it is time to learn about each other, the challenges faced by your team and how to grow your leadership.

- *Limit status reporting to five minutes:* If you must cover status, do it quickly. Better to submit a bulleted summary or a dashboard than waste precious time reviewing each project.

- *Share success, not problems:* Be sure to celebrate at least one success in your time together. Your boss will appreciate hearing good news for a change. Kick off your agenda with a success story. The resulting energy will set the tone for the rest of the meeting. That way you both leave the meeting with a great buzz!

- *Present your ideas and get your boss's reaction:* Prove to your boss that you can solve issues. Rather than asking him or her what they think you should do about a particular issue, offer a suggestion. Then, discuss it openly—the pros and the cons. It's easier for a boss to respond to a suggestion than to delve into the detail and then come up with an answer himself.

- *Plan your next team meeting:* Together, brainstorm the needs you see in the team.

- *Perform a goal check:* You probably set goals at the beginning of the year. Talk about them! Discuss your progress and don't wait for half the year to go by!

- *Discuss rumours:* You hear them though your boss might not. It's good to get them out in the open since many of them turn out to be true. Discuss how best to deal with the rumour mill and how to present a united front.

- *Don't complain:* Remember there's probably someone out there right now being critical of your leadership! Try to develop yourself as a leader, not a complainer.

- *Review strengths:* Share what is currently energising you at work. Discuss how you might be able to create more of that energy on a daily basis.

- *Ask for feedback:* Avoid general questions like 'How am I doing?' It's too vague and it beckons an open response. Go for something more actionable and specific.

- *Relax:* Spend time connecting with your supervisor. Be a person, not a boss or employee. Get to know who they are. Let them know you. You may be surprised that the both of you end up looking forward to your one-on-ones!

7

Participation, Presentation And Influencing Skills

Now, let us look at ways in which each individual taking part in a meeting can contribute most effectively.

We also consider *presentation skills*—how to make your point clearly and with maximum impact. Then, we look at *influencing skills*—using your understanding of the meeting and its members to act as a 'vice chairperson', inspiring constructive discussion and discouraging inappropriate behaviour amongst your colleagues.

EFFECTIVE PARTICIPATION

Be Prepared

Preparation is vital. Spend as much time as possible becoming familiar with the background to any meeting you attend.

- Are there any papers or minutes which you should read or absorb?
- Who will be there?

- What sort of common ground will there be between you and the other participants?
- How can you go about establishing shared interests before the meeting?

Be Punctual

Make sure you know exactly where the meeting is being held and leave enough time to get there. Don't let yourself be distracted by last-minute telephone calls or conversations. Being late will put you at an immediate disadvantage—not only will you appear disorganised to the other participants but you may have missed important information. You could then spend the rest of the meeting frantically trying to catch up, potentially missing further relevant points in the process.

Be Alert

Do adopt a positive and alert posture during the meeting. Don't:

- stare into space.
- slouch.
- fidget.
- look as though you are merely paying lip service to somebody's opinions while you wait for your say.

By your approach, you should convey to the other members of the meeting that you are really paying attention, concentrating hard on what other people are saying. Then, when you are speaking, they will naturally listen more attentively to your views if they feel you have given them a fair hearing.

Be Positive

Always look for what's positive about the meeting or what someone is saying rather than focusing on what's negative, or allowing your personal antipathy towards a colleague make you dismiss their comments out of hand. If your reservations are justified, they will be more convincingly put across through a reasoned approach than by resorting to dogma or obvious prejudice.

Be Involved

Do seek to be the kind of participant you would expect others to be. The more attention you pay, and the more you are seen to pay:

- the more you will gain from the meeting.
- the more the meeting will reflect positively on you and your professional approach.

GENERAL PRESENTATION SKILLS

It is a natural tendency to assume that everything you say at a meeting will be interpreted in precisely the way that you want it to be by everyone else present. Unfortunately, the potential for misunderstanding and misinterpretation is considerable.

Preparation and care in the way you present yourself at meetings is important if you really want to be heard and be a part of facilitating change.

Timing

It is often an irresistible temptation to introduce ideas or opinions into the meeting as soon as they occur to you. Not only is this likely to disrupt the flow of the discussion, it may also mean that perfectly valid ideas are stillborn through being introduced before their natural time. An effective participant will time his or her contributions for the point in the meeting where they are most appropriate.

Judgement

A key skill is that of being able to listen carefully to the discussion and judge the stage the meeting is at, at any particular time. Each agenda item can go through a cycle of phases, such as:

- defining the problem,
- collecting information,
- defining the next step,
- taking action,
- analysing what happened, and
- drawing out principles for potential future use.

Signal Your Attention

When you feel that the time is appropriate for you to make a point, you should try to lead into it in some way, so that you have engaged the meeting's attention before you reach the crux of the matter, for instance: 'I'd like to ask a question about...'

This effectively signals your intention. Once your 'audience' is listening, you can be sure they will absorb most of what you are saying, rather than missing the first sentence or so. You will also have gained a little extra time to compose your thoughts, should you need it.

MAKING A FORMAL PRESENTATION

At some time or other, you may find yourself required to make a formal presentation of some kind at a meeting. Whether this takes less than two minutes, or over half-an-hour, certain principles remain the same. The following three steps will make your presentation more effective.

- Plan what you want to say, to whom and when.

- Prepare how you propose to say it, including use of visual aids.

- Practice, that is, rehearse before the event with a 'walk-through' of the presentation. It is better to identify and overcome problems at this stage than on the day of the meeting.

Planning

There are three key elements to consider, all at once, for effective planning, which can be summed up by the mnemonic **'OAC'**.

'O' for outcome/objectives

What are you hoping to achieve by the end of the presentation? It is useful to imagine people's likely reactions to what you say and, more importantly, how you say it.

'A' for audience

Who is the presentation aimed at? You can develop a summary by considering another three 'A's.

Aims: What sort of expectations will the audience have in listening to you? Will they be more interested in short- or long-term implications? Are there any vested interests? Are you likely to get a fair hearing?

Aspirations/ambitions: What do they hope to achieve, and what efforts are they prepared to make in that direction? What suggested outcome will most appeal to them?

Assumptions: Are they likely to have any preconceptions about you and your role? May they even be suspicious of your motives? Even if you are not particularly familiar with the other participants, you may be able to get some clues to their attitudes by speaking with their colleagues or associates beforehand.

By following this process, you should gain a clearer understanding of the people to whom your presentation will be directed. This will not only help you assess what they will respond to, but also help you identify possible points that need pre-emptive action.

'C' for content

How will your planning of the outcome and your understanding of the audience affect the content of your presentation? Once you have established the content, you may need to reassess your expectations of the outcome or, perhaps, ask further questions about your audience.

OAC is often not a straight-forward progress from *Outcome* to *Audience* to *Content*—you may find yourself repeating steps or going back and forth, from one to another, to achieve an optimum result.

Preparation

You can now start to plan the way in which you will present the ideas or information that you need to put across. Your presentation must gain the attention of your audience from the outset, giving them an overview of what you are going to say, and if necessary telling them what sort of involvement you expect from them—when they can ask questions, for example.

A useful tip is to prepare the first few sentences carefully, to gain maximum impact. Every audience will give you at least thirty seconds at the start—while they make up their minds about whether they want to pay attention to what you have to say. It will help if you can start by outlining how many key points you are going to make. You can then use this number as a 'map' of the presentation.

For example:

'Now that I've finished with the third point, we can concentrate on the fourth, which is quite controversial.'

Good presentations should leave people inspired, motivated and empowered to act effectively on what has been decided. If you can find a suitably positive or encouraging note to end on—one which will mean something to that particular audience—you are more likely to engage them in achieving the stated objectives.

Rehearsal

The amount of rehearsal that you need to do for a presentation will obviously depend on your familiarity with the subject and the complexity of the content. It is possible, however, to over-rehearse—which will result in a rather stiff, laboured presentation.

Although it is important to know your subject thoroughly, your prepared material should really only be a series of key points—leaving adequate room for you to put them across with a degree of spontaneity.

Over-preparation leaves little or no scope for useful variations or digressions.

Persuasion

If the objective of the presentation is to persuade the participants to follow a particular course of action or adopt a particular approach, it is good to start with an acknowledgement of all their likely objections. Unless such negative points are brought out into the open, the participants will not accept that you have really understood their point of view. Facing such objections head on will at least give your proposals a degree of credibility, and also provide you with the opportunity to take pre-emptive action.

Pacing Yourself

Getting the timing right can be a critical factor at meetings. Overrunning may make it appear that you have been 'waffling', whereas 'drying up' after only a quarter of your allotted time can make you look incompetent or ill-prepared. Of these two faults, the most common is for people to include too much material and overrun. It is also worth leaving adequate time for discussion or question-and-answer session, where appropriate.

PRESENTATION SKILLS

Basically, your most important technique is being yourself. No specific 'trick' or technique will be effective unless you have integrated it into your own personal style. Sincerity and enthusiasm are infectious and will always get conveyed to your audience. They will more readily identify with these characteristics than any amount of high-flown theory or technique.

By being yourself, you are taking an honest and open approach that will make your audience far more ready to trust you, or feel some affinity with your opinions. Also, as we have already seen, if you know enough about them to understand their attitudes and perceptions, you will be able to present things in a manner to which they can readily relate.

Eye Contact

The more directly you look at the members of your audience, the more likely you are to build some sort of rapport. Eye-to-eye contact can be a most successful way of conveying self-assurance (if you are not sure of what you are saying, they are certainly unlikely to be convinced by it) and honesty (a direct approach signifies that you have nothing to hide).

In the context of a large meeting, it will obviously be impossible for you to establish eye contact with everyone present. Nevertheless, remember that it should not be limited to looking at:

- an unspecified area six inches above everyone's heads.
- your notes or, in extreme cases, your shoes.
- the most influential person in the meeting.
- the most friendly face in the meeting.

Appearance

In the early stages of a presentation, your appearance will be crucial to your credibility. As with most other things, your audience will all have different expectations about dress and draw their own inference as to what it signifies.

What one person sees as a smart, obviously authoritative figure, another will see as a stiff-collared busybody with no conception of life at the 'sharp end' of the company.

When you are working in an unfamiliar setting, therefore, it is prudent to find out something about the dress code for the meeting. Being smartly dressed is generally good policy, but being appropriately dressed for your audience and location is more important.

INFLUENCING SKILLS

To influence the meeting, you must first acknowledge the role of the psychological and political undercurrents that may be present and then the techniques and manoeuvres used to exploit them. The following are examples of some of the most common ways in which people seek to influence meetings.

Keeping Key Issues Away From A Particular Meeting

This well-known tactic is often used when someone believes their idea will be opposed or even defeated if submitted to a meeting. Major items are fixed beforehand, the meeting itself is a sham and the minutes are doctored. An item can be excluded from successive meetings until it becomes too late to find an alternative.

Lobbying

Successful influencing can begin well before the meeting itself. Analyse previous trends, interests, how power is exercised and by whom, and outcomes. You can then ascertain support for a contentious item before it comes in for discussion.

Recognition Of Power

Some or all of the sources of power identified below may be at work in any meeting. Understanding them and how they affect participants' behaviour is a necessary skill for anyone seeking to be more influential at meetings.

- *Expert power:* It is conferred on people thought to have specialised knowledge. The important point to remember is that their power depends not necessarily on their actual knowledge, but on the perceptions of other people.

- *Reward power:* It exists when an individual has the power to reward someone for compliance with their instructions. The reward may be money, promotion, responsibility or support for a chosen course of action.

- *Coercion power:* Almost the reverse of reward power, it is the ability to punish by withdrawal of favours, friendship or emotional support.

- *Reference power:* It is otherwise known as power through charisma or personality. This individual can inspire and persuade others to comply with his or her wishes.

'Hidden' Agenda

The hidden agenda consists of issues that are not on the agenda, which concern the participants as much as, or more than, those issues which are. The hidden agenda will rarely be overtly discussed at the meeting, although it will influence the way the meeting is conducted and the participants' behaviour.

Participants under a threat of redundancy, for instance, will not behave objectively—they will not be honest and they will be suspicious of one another. Upon the removal of the threat, people will again be able to trust each other.

Other Forms Of Coercion

Pressure put on some participants by their colleagues in order to secure a particular outcome is another manifestation of the hidden agenda. To dispel it, identify the strategies in use and confront the perpetrators with what is actually going on. Remove the element of secrecy so that the issues can be discussed in an open and positive way.

STEERING THE MEETING

Everyone has the potential to influence a meeting, irrespective of their role. There is no reason why the chairperson should take all the initiatives or do all the work.

Anyone can steer the meeting by being aware of its processes. Are the participants listening, giving their full attention to the topic, or arguing? If the chairperson does not or cannot intervene, there are a number of approaches you can take yourself.

- **Bringing in others:** Invite an opinion from someone who is not being given an opportunity to contribute.

   'You have not spoken so far, what would you like to say something about this proposal?'

- **Relieving tension:** Restore a sense of proportion or add a touch of humour.

'If the competition could see us now, they'd have a good laugh!'

- **Mediating:** Acknowledge and reconcile other people's views.

'X and Y clearly want the same outcome for the department, but probably by using different methods. Perhaps, they could each explain the advantages of their own proposals.'

- **Summarising:** Remind people of the stage they have reached.

'It seems to me that the last five minutes have brought forward three new ideas that need to be considered as follows...'

- **Dramatic movements:** Stand up abruptly, knocking back your chair. You now have (hopefully) gained the meeting's attention and have the opportunity to remind them of their real objective.

'What are we trying to achieve at present?'

- **Increase the irrelevancies:** In the face of an increasingly irrelevant debate, exaggerate the flow by making progressively more meaningless remarks until it becomes obvious to all concerned. This is an ideal point for you to ask: 'What are we here for, anyway?'

- **Leaving quietly:** This is effective when there is an argument between two or more people on a particular issue. Without saying anything at all, get up and quietly leave. When you next see the people concerned, you can explain why you behaved as you did, or you can pointedly remind participants that if the same thing happens again you have no intention of staying.

- **'Ten minutes more':** Announce in a loud voice that you have 'only ten more minutes' before you have to leave. Ask: 'What are we hoping to achieve in that time?' Make sure you do leave once the time is up.

  These interventions are designed to gain the meeting's attention in an unusual way, with the purpose of steering it in a different direction. A lot depends on how accurately you assess the mood of the meeting and how dramatically you perform.

8

Review And Follow-Up

Very few organisations take the trouble to work out the actual cost of their meetings. For instance, bringing together senior managers for protracted periods of time can prove surprisingly expensive, merely in terms of salary—not to mention the background planning and preparation necessary. For more prestigious meetings, there could well be travel, hotel and conferencing expenses to take into account as well.

The immediate financial demands are relatively simple to quantify. However, it is more difficult to ascertain the effectiveness of the meeting in improving efficiency or productivity for the future. Remember that if you waste time, you also waste money.

The follow-up steps described below are designed to provide ways to evaluate the number and type of meetings you hold, with the intention of streamlining the process, holding fewer, more effective meetings and consequently running a more motivated, cost-effective operation.

INDIVIDUAL MEETING REVIEW

At the end of each meeting, allocate a short period for each participant to comment on how the meeting was run and suggest possible improvements. Attentive listening and careful recording is important for this approach, so that small but potentially significant changes are acknowledged and acted upon.

Extend this approach to encourage participants to write down their thoughts and forward them to the chairperson, or whoever is managing the review procedure. A few simple questions are enough to yield worthwhile results.

- How clear were the objectives of the meeting?

- Was the agenda made available in good time?

- How satisfied were you with the outcome of the meeting?

For clarity and ease of use, it may be useful for the answers to be graded on a scale, for instance:

Not at all...1...2...3...4...5...6...7...8...9... Completely

When this procedure has been in place for a while—and if it seems to be yielding useful results—think about introducing more difficult types of questions with more illuminating results. For instance, how effective was the chairperson in handling the agenda? Clearly, this requires a chairperson who is prepared to consider potentially critical comments about his or her performance.

Develop written feedback, still further, via the inclusion of a number of open-ended questions. Utilising, as they do, participants' personal thoughts, these could give a deeper insight into those factors which are preventing the meeting from functioning satisfactorily, for instance, what in your view are the major factors which prevent the meeting from being more effective?

Meeting Review Procedure

The following questionnaire is to be completed by all the participants at the meeting. The total number of marks for each item are added up to represent the overall rating from everyone in attendance. Items with the lowest scores can then be discussed and action agreed on as to how to improve the meeting in these areas.

Meeting review sheet (each item to be marked out of 10)

Are our meetings necessary?

Are our meetings useful?

Do we meet at the right frequency?

Are our meetings of the right duration?

Do the right people attend?

Are our agendas appropriate?

Do we have the necessary information?

Do we have effective decision-making procedures?

Do we make the right use of external help?

Is our meeting room adequate?

Do we use appropriate aids?

Do we keep appropriate records?

Is the timekeeping satisfactory?

Are potential interruptions handled correctly?

Are refreshment arrangements adequate?

Is the room laid out correctly?

Do we review our performance effectively?

| Do we learn from our mistakes? |
| Do we take action as a result of performance reviews? |

Audit Of Meetings

Just as any organisation carries out a financial audit, a similar procedure can be applied to examine the number and types of meetings held. It is then possible to assess whether the time and effort—and therefore money—currently devoted to organising and attending meetings is justified. Are the meetings a cost-effective process to achieve the desired outcomes?

The auditing process has three stages.

Types and number of meetings

This information may require some investigation as informal (unrecorded) meetings can easily require it. An attempt should be made to classify the nature and purpose of each meeting.

Aims, objectives and outcomes

What kind of meetings (staff, policy, board, etc.) are they? What are their aims and objectives? Are these aims and objectives sufficiently communicated to everyone who attends? It is useful to devise a simple questionnaire to gauge participants' individual reactions.

Evaluating their effectiveness

Once the objectives of each meeting have been clarified, their actual outcomes can be used to form a view of their successes.

Where it becomes apparent that meetings have fallen some way short of achieving their objectives, you should take steps to find out why. Again, it can be useful to devise a simple questionnaire to assess individual reactions. Did the right people attend the meeting? Who was left out and in what areas did this create a deficiency or imbalance? Where there were personality clashes and could these have been avoided with more careful preparation or a more perceptive or capable chairperson?

Outsider Review

To make rapid progress in improving meetings across the whole organisation, it can be useful to use an outsider—anyone not familiar with your way of working—to act as a 'coach'. Someone taking on this role would initially sit in a corner and observe the proceedings closely, if necessary making notes on what people say and do.

After the meeting is over, a process review can be conducted with the participants, about how they perceived that particular meeting and how it could be improved. Confronting the meeting with questions rather than telling the participants what they have to do may prove fruitful. The aim should be focused on helping the meeting to discover what they have to change to improve.

Continuing Development Of Meetings

The involvement of an outsider should always be seen as helping the meeting process to help itself. As quickly as possible, the coach should try to shift the responsibility for improvement back to the in-house participants themselves.

As we have seen, one way of doing this is to encourage the chairperson to include a 'Review of the Meeting' in the agenda. Once this is working well, participants can be encouraged to consider ways in which the meeting could be improved for the future—not merely the current decisions and process, but in any way whatsoever.

It is important to decide on the action required to improve the conduct of the meeting. This crucial step is rarely taken. Too often meetings have analysed what is not working, and this knowledge is shared by every participant, yet nothing is done to change things.

Drawing lessons or principles to guide future meetings, which are both practical and accepted by everyone, is the first important step forward. These new principles or procedures can then themselves be reviewed after a period of time, leading to new methods of working and an approach that can be termed 'continuous improvement' or 'learning to learn'.

As the saying goes: A thousand-mile journey begins with the first step!

Minutes of meetings

The minutes of the meeting should be written by the meeting secretary as soon as possible, while the subjects are still fresh in the minds of both the secretary and the members. The minutes should be a brief but accurate account of the business transacted at the meeting.

In order to ensure an efficient business organisation, each meeting should be identifiable (by a reference number, for example) and a permanent record of the following items should be made.

- Where and when the meeting was held?

- Who chaired the meeting?

- Who was present?

- Who sent their apologies, if absent?

- A statement that the agenda was adhered to, example that the minutes of the previous meeting were agreed and signed.

- A few lines summarising reports, including file numbers, so that members can obtain copies if they wish.

- A summary of any discussion that followed the reports

- All motions and amendments in the exact form they were put up by the chairperson

- The names of the proposer and seconder of each motion and amendment

- A summary of the main points of the discussion

- The number of those who voted

- The decision taken on each proposal

- Who is taking what action and when?

- The date of the next meeting

The secretary's task in writing the minutes of the meeting is to convey the flavour of the meeting and strength of opinion of the participants to those people who were unable to attend. People who did attend need to have confirmation of what they and their colleagues discussed and decided. This prevents subsequent arguments about what was actually agreed.

It is advisable to develop an impersonal style, avoiding dialogue or quoting from long-winded speeches. By doing this, you will ensure the facts are clear and not masked by unnecessary detail. Reduce long discussions to clear statements of the main points, which contain the essentials and avoid the 'waffle'.

Sometimes people adopt the procedure at the meeting itself. In this case, the chairperson sums up the main arguments of the discussion, states the decision agreed upon, the participants' action, saying who does what and when. The secretary will then read back what the chairperson has dictated. Usually the group will confirm them without further discussion.

After The Meeting

A copy of the minutes should be sent to everybody who has a right or need to know as soon as possible. If writing the minutes is likely to be delayed, then some sort of interim action sheet should be sent.

The chairperson normally has the opportunity to check the minutes before they are sent out. In this way, minor errors can be eliminated and misunderstanding can be avoided.

The writing of minutes can all too easily be seen as thankless drudgery but their role should not be overlooked. Accurate and timely minutes are essential to the overall progress and results of any regular meeting or committee.

How to wreck meetings

It is interesting to look at the ways that meetings can be wrecked, so that those of you who wish to spot the tactic being used can take these methods into account. The following list is by no means exhaustive. So many of the words that start with 'D', **defeat** the meeting.

- *Distract and disrupt:* Make a loud noise, talk about anything off the point, bring in subjects that are irrelevant, generally offer advice where it is not needed.

- *Disagree:* Beg to differ, perhaps politely, but find ways of disagreeing with the main thrusts of everyone else's argument. Disagree on principle, disagree on fact and disagree with emotion.

- *Defend and attack:* Related to number 2 is the use of defence and attack. Attack the people with whom you disagree and when they attack back defend even more vigorously. If you have the skill, introduce a hint of paranoia—that always seems to attract a decent crowd.

- *Dominate:* Push your own points at the expense of others. If you have a powerful voice, use it. If not wave your arms about, shuffle your papers, lean over and point at someone else's papers, but generally impose yourself on the meeting and ensure that no one else gets the same degree of time and space as you.

- *Deviate:* Refer back to previous meetings when you did not get your way and say why you feel you should be recompensed. Tell people that this situation reminds you of that time back in 1986 when you were Head of Public Relations for…and if your reminiscences don't work, try to get someone else reminiscing—preferably the oldest and most sentimental participant at the meeting.

- *Divide*: Ensure that you have spoken to each of the different lobby groups before the meeting and said different things to each one. Try to set one lobby against another and then sit back and watch the fun as matters move on.

- *Deride*: Generally imply that one or other member of the meeting is not quite telling the honest truth. Lines such as 'But we all know what can be done with statistics like these' will cause enough of a stir.

- *Dubious data*: This is a particularly effective way of ruining a meeting with scientists and engineers. They tend to like data and factual arguments. So give them data and facts, but don't worry about whether any of them are accurate or not. Wave statistics, graphs and charts around. When challenged, imply that these are early provisional results and that a more detailed survey is being carried out. That should delay things by several months.

- *Damn with faint praise:* If someone uses the 'dubious data technique' on you then apply a serious and knowing eye to ripping the data apart. Say that the data they are quoting comes from material that was relevant ten years ago but things have changed now. Doubt the credibility of the people who collected the data, doubt the sanity of the people who added it up.

- *Baiting or corporate wind-up:* It is when marketing gets back at personnel for all those appraisals, or production gets back at finance for all those forms, or just about anyone gets back at corporate planning.

MEETING REVIEW

A group training exercise: Agree/Disagree statements

- Meetings are nearly always a waste of time. A D

- People attending a meeting should be encouraged to participate. A D

- The success of meetings depends upon a strong chairperson. A D

- The best number of members at a meeting is between five and seven. A D

- No concern need be felt about silent members on a committee, since their silence is invariably the result of agreement with what is being said. A D

- A meeting where all contributions are invited and then addressed to the chairperson is usually efficient and productive. A D

- If meetings are to be held regularly, it is a good idea to rotate the chairperson's role among the members of the group. A D

- The chairperson's attitude to the meeting will be reflected in the attitudes of the group members to each other. A D

- When the chairperson is doing his or her best, one should not openly criticise or find fault with their conduct. A D

- Generally there comes a time when democratic group methods must be abandoned in order to solve practical problems.   A   D

- It is sometimes necessary to ignore the feelings of others in order to reach a group decision.   A   D

- In a decision-taking meeting too much emphasis is placed on whether the members are happy with the outcome, as opposed to whether the decision is the best one.   A   D

- There would be more attentiveness in meetings if the chairperson would get to the point quickly and say what he or she wants the others to do.   A   D

- A meeting functions most efficiently when it ignores rather than discusses rivalries between members.   A   D

- The typical meeting would be improved if the chairperson imposed firm discipline on the proceedings.   A   D

9

Win-Win Meetings

Sometimes meetings fail when matters come to a loggerhead and proceedings come to a standstill. It is time to implement the skills of negotiation to turn it into a win-win situation.

Effective negotiation helps you resolve situations, where what you want conflicts with what someone else wants. The aim of a win-win negotiation is to find a solution that is acceptable to both parties, and leaves both parties feeling that they've won.

There are different styles of negotiation, depending on circumstances.

Where you do not expect to deal with people ever again and you do not need their goodwill, then it may be appropriate to 'play hardball', seeking to win a negotiation while the other person loses out.

Similarly, where there is a great deal at stake in a negotiation, then it may be appropriate to prepare in detail and legitimate 'gamesmanship' to gain advantage.

Neither of these approaches is usually quite good for resolving disputes with people with whom you have an ongoing relationship. Using tricks and manipulation during a negotiation can undermine trust and damage teamwork. While a manipulative person may not get caught out if negotiation is infrequent, this is not the case when people work together routinely. Here, honesty and openness are almost always the best policies.

Preparing For A Successful Negotiation

Depending on the scale of the disagreement, some preparation may be appropriate for conducting a successful negotiation. For small disagreements, excessive preparation can be counter-productive because it takes time. It can also be seen as manipulative.

If you need to resolve a major disagreement, then make sure you prepare thoroughly. Think through the following points.

Goals: What do you want to get out of the negotiation? What do you think the other person wants?

Trades: What do you and the other person have that you can trade? What do you each have that the other wants? What are you and the other person comfortable giving away?

Alternatives: If you don't reach an agreement with the other person, what alternatives do you have? Are these good or bad? How much does it matter to you if you do not reach an agreement? Does failure to reach an agreement remove future opportunities? And what alternatives might the other person have?

Relationships: What is the history of the relationship? Could or should this history impact the negotiation? Will there be any hidden issues that may influence the negotiation? How will you handle these?

Expected outcomes: What outcome will people be expecting from this negotiation? What has the outcome been in the past and what precedents have been set?

Consequences: What are the consequences for you of winning or losing this negotiation? What are the consequences for the other person?

Power: Who has what power in the relationship? Who controls resources? Who stands to lose the most if an agreement isn't reached? What power does the other person have to deliver?

Possible solutions

Based on all above considerations, what possible compromises might there be?

Style is critical: For a negotiation to be a 'win-win', both parties should feel positive about the negotiation once it's over. This helps people keep good working relationships afterwards. This governs the style of the negotiation— histrionics. Display of emotion is clearly inappropriate because they undermine the rational basis of negotiation.

TWELVE MANTRAS

- Think of the long-term mutual gain instead of the short-time personal gain. A win-win negotiation means a shared benefit. Forget about your own personal gain and concentrate on what will make both sides happy.

- Set a trusting, cooperative tone for the meeting right from the beginning. A win-win situation can be built on a foundation of trust and shared respect.

- Do your homework.

- Discuss the issues using first-person plural pronouns.

- Focus on interests, not positions.

- Increase the number of issues you negotiate.

- Avoid ultimatums.

- Give to get.

- Maintain your composure and objectivity. If you become angry, you lose.

- Engage in creative problem-solving.

- Keep searching for ways to add value. Leave out no possibility to find ways to increase the value of what the other person wants.

- Document all agreements.